Longman
Proficiency Skills
Coursebook

Roy Kingsbury and Mary Spratt

Keeping — Howard.

Longman

Longman Group Limited,
Longman House, Burnt Mill, Harlow,
Essex CM20 2JE, England
and Associated Companies throughout the world.

First published 1984
Second impression 1985
ISBN 0 582 55938 3

Set in 9 on 11pt Monophoto Helvetica

Printed and bound in Spain by
TONSA, San Sebastian

Contents

Introduction to the Student

Who Proficiency Skills is for

Longman Proficiency Skills is designed specifically for students preparing for the Cambridge Certificate of Proficiency in English Examination. You should really have already done an advanced course before starting this one.

The aims of Proficiency Skills

To familiarise you with the content and aims of all five Papers in the Proficiency Exam.

To give you training in the language and skills required for the exam and for mastery of a foreign language.

To present you with the range of topics, text types and styles of language that are likely to occur in the exam.

To provide you with an interesting, enjoyable and stimulating course of study.

The organisation of the contents of Proficiency Skills

This book contains 15 Units + a complete Proficiency Practice Exam – as you can see on the opposite page.

Remember that the revised Proficiency Examination consists of five Papers:

Paper 1: Reading Comprehension (1 hour)
Paper 2: Composition (2 hours)
Paper 3: Use of English (2 hours)
Paper 4: Listening Comprehension (20–30 minutes)
Paper 5: Interview (12–15 minutes)

Each Paper is prepared for three times in the book, as follows:

Paper 1 Reading Comprehension: Units 1, 6 and 11
Paper 2 Composition: Units 2, 7 and 12
Paper 3 Use of English: Units 3, 8 and 13
Paper 4 Listening Comprehension: Units 4, 9 and 14
Paper 5 Interview: Units 5, 10 and 15

Each Unit focuses specifically on a particular Paper BUT at the same time also includes Discussion, Grammar, Vocabulary, Listening, Role play and so on.

How you can help yourself to learn inside the classroom

This course is *not* a set of practice exams or test papers disguised as a course. It helps you by giving you both language and skills guidance which in the classroom will often involve you in pair and group work, discussions and analyses as well as listening tasks, note-taking and so on. So be prepared to take part! Participating fully in all the classroom learning activities will enable you to gain most benefit from this course and enjoy your learning.

How you can help yourself to learn outside the classroom

No course on its own can prepare you fully for the Cambridge Proficiency Examination. You must be prepared to read and listen to as much English as possible in your spare time. Also make time to do more homework than the amount suggested in the course, and when doing set course homework train yourself to keep to the 'recommended time'.

Enjoy the course, and good luck with the exam!

Roy Kingsbury and Mary Spratt

Skills and Language Content

Unit	Proficiency Paper	Exam Skills	Language Grammar	Vocabulary
1	Reading Comprehension	Five reading skills	Inversion constructions	Guessing the meaning of words from context
2	Composition	Discursive composition planning and writing	Verb + noun/pronoun/ possessive adj. + gerund	Sentence joining words
3	Use of English	Summary writing, and completing blanks in passages	The use or absence of definite article *the*	Sentence joining words (in summary writing)
4	Listening Comprehension	Accents, interpreting graphs, charts, etc., and predicting	Some adjective and adverb constructions	Adverb-adjective collocations
5	Interview	Talking about a photo, and reading aloud	Relative pronouns, and uses of participle *-ing* form	Expressions used in discussion, and compound nouns
6	Reading Comprehension	Multiple-choice questions, and vocabulary building	Present Perfect, Simple Past and Past Perfect	Differences in meaning, collocation, and vocabulary areas
7	Composition	'Directed writing' compositions, and style	Various uses of modal verbs (+ 'modal' nouns)	Expressions of approval and disapproval
8	Use of English	Answering questions on a passage, and explaining phrases	Passive constructions	Nouns from phrasal verbs
9	Listening Comprehension	Multiple-choice questions: reading, predicting, answering	Formal and informal reporting	Reporting verbs; and adjectives to report emotions, feelings, etc.
10	Interview	Talking about a photo, reading aloud, discussion	Variations on standard 'if'-clauses	Related nouns and verbs differentiated by stress or pronunciation
11	Reading Comprehension	Author's style and attitude; word connotations	Units 11–15 contain no sections or phases which concentrate on specific areas of grammar or vocabulary. Instead, the second half of each of these Units provides explicit Exam Guidance and Exam Advice.	
12	Composition	Descriptive and narrative composition planning and writing		
13	Use of English	Completing blanks in sentences and dialogues	**The Exam Guidance** in each Unit takes the form of typical Proficiency Paper questions with expected, suggested or possible answers together with reasons and comments, and is intended for classroom use.	
14	Listening Comprehension	Dealing with speakers' moods, feelings, attitudes and register	**The Exam Advice** aims to give clear tips on what to do and what not to do when you sit each Paper.	
15	Interview	Talking about a photo, reading aloud, participating in role play and discussion		
COMPLETE PROFICIENCY PRACTICE EXAM				

1 Heredity or Environment?

1 Look at the headline and picture opposite. Can you predict from the two what the following article will be about? Note down your predictions, then compare them with other students'.

2 Read quickly through the article (without paying attention to detail) to see which predictions were most accurate.

3 Now read the article again, this time much more carefully, to look for information in answer to these questions:

1 What is John Stroud's connection with twins separated at birth or soon after?
2 How interested would Thomas Bouchard have been in studying Romulus and Remus?
3 Why is the period from 1927 to the 1950s of particular interest to those wishing to study twins of this particular kind?

4 Why, in Britain nowadays, is it easier than previously for adopted childen to discover their real parents?
5 Why does Stroud no longer use the telephone to tell people his news about them?
6 To what degree does Stroud consider his work to have been successful?

4 Vocabulary

Find the following words in the article. Then in pairs try to work out their meaning as used in the article by looking at the general meaning of the words surrounding each:

Paragraph 1: odds; painstaking
Paragraph 2: dwelt
Paragraph 3: fodder; nurture
Paragraph 6: inkling; marginally
Paragraph 7: sibling; startling

5 Discussion

In small groups, discuss these questions:

1 Do you approve of researchers informing people that they were adopted and that they have a twin sister or brother they have never known about?
2 Do you think Bouchard's research may prove useful? If so, how? And to whom?
3 Nature or Nurture? Heredity or Environment? In your opinion, which is most important in determining a person's character?

'According to the guidebook, they've now discovered that it was in fact a he-wolf that reared them.'

How divided twins grew up alike

The odds across the human race of producing identical twins are 240 to one against. John Stroud is a social worker who deals in still longer odds: finding pairs of twins separated at birth or soon after and reuniting them in middle age, often to the earth-shaking astonishment of at least one of the parties concerned. Since 1960 Stroud has, by patient and painstaking detective work, reunited 26 pairs of twins, and in a great many cases one of the parties had not the faintest idea they were one of a pair. The discovery has usually, but not always, been a joy.

Twins are fascinating in their similarities and the richness of coincidence in their separate lives. Yet they need not be at all alike, whether merely fraternal or biologically identical; Esau was 'a hairy man and a fine hunter', while Jacob was 'a smooth and quiet man who dwelt in tents'. Nor, as the same pair proved, need twins be the best of friends.

But Jacob and Esau, like Romulus and Remus, were raised together, whether by their natural parents or a she-wolf. Twins reared apart are rich research fodder for those who try to determine why we are as we are, and whether our character is set by heredity or environment, the endless question of nature versus nurture. They are a select group who share identical heredity but different environments.

Such pairs re-joined by Stroud have been seized upon by Professor Thomas Bouchard of the University of Minnesota in Minneapolis, who since 1979 has been engaged in just such a study, based upon the few pairs of separately-reared twins available to him. Nearly half his subjects have come from England.

Such pairs are relatively rare, because there are few good reasons for separating infant twins. In times past the unwanted, the illegitimate and the orphaned would in all probability have been sent to the workhouse together, and for the past 30 years few adoption societies will have dreamed of placing pairs in separate adoptive homes. But there was a period in England when it did occasionally happen, between the introduction of legal adoption in 1927 and the dawn of enlightenment upon the social services in the 1950s.

Reunification depends upon one half of the pair knowing, or at least suspecting, that they are a twin; it must be presumed that there are a number alive who have no inkling. Changes in the law that allow adopted children to discover their real roots have stirred interest and made the task marginally easier. Adopted children can at least track down their original birth certificates.

But for Stroud, the biggest problem of all is how to break the news to the lost sibling. He long ago gave up the direct telephone call in favour of a discreetly worded letter which asks if he can call to see them on 'a very confidential matter'. It is, after all, rather startling news if you are not expecting it.

But the outcome has, on the whole, been a happy one. Stroud estimates that, among his 26 successful pairings, in only three or four cases has the relationship cooled rapidly after the first meeting, for reasons as many as the numbers involved. But, he says, none would have missed the experience; they all needed it to get at the truth of their own lives.

Reading Skills

There are several different reading skills which you will be expected to handle in the Proficiency Examination. If you can't handle these skills in the exam, you may well waste time or get your answers wrong, or both.

Think about the tasks you did in exercises 1–4 on pp. 6–7. Did you read in the same way to find the answers? Perhaps you can already say what reading skills you employed for each task.

Here we are going to study and practise five reading skills in connection with the text below.

---

1 | **Skimming**

'Skimming' is introductory reading. It means reading something over very quickly just to find out what it is generally about – to get the 'gist' of it. To do this kind of reading efficiently, it is important *not* to read the text in detail.

'Skim' the article below in about a minute and answer this one question:

What's the article about?

Eugene Evans expects to receive £35,000 this year as a computer program designer with a small computer software company in Liver-
5 pool. He would be an unremarkable high-flying professional were he not aged only 16.

Other executives of his calibre and earning power might well own a
10 Jaguar and a detached bungalow in half an acre, and take an annual holiday in Barbados.

But when you are 16, you have to be fetched by taxi for work every day, 15 because you are too young to drive, and you have to hand over £20 a week housekeeping money to your mother.

A year ago, he was sitting behind a
20 school desk studying for six 'O' Levels and two CSEs; computer studies was not even on the curriculum.

He is entirely self-taught, having read books on computers beneath
25 the bedclothes from the age of 12, and has made himself an expert in writing games of the *Star Wars* variety, said to be one of the most difficult tasks in computer software.
30   He designed his first program 'Space Panic', last year. Shortly afterwards, the company Image Software was launched and invited him to become an employee. His basic
35 salary is £17,000, and he makes as much again in bonuses, bringing work home at night.

His earnings this year are likely to be seven times those of his father, a
40 bus driver in Liverpool. Far from being jealous, his father is delighted.

2 | Scanning

'Scanning' is reading to find the whereabouts of very specific information, e.g. dates, figures, names, or answers to questions. To scan properly you needn't, in fact *mustn't* read everything, but just look for the required information. It's like looking for a number in a telephone directory.

'Scan' the article for the following information. Write the line references and your answers on a piece of paper.

1 Eugene's expected salary this year: _35,000 £_
2 Eugene's age: _16_
3 The car older people in his profession might own: _Jaguar_
4 The number of 'O' Levels he has: _6_
5 The age at which he started reading about computers: _12_
6 The name of his first computer program: _Space panic_
7 His basic salary: _17,000_
8 The name of his firm: _Image software_
9 The place where his father works: _Liverpool_
10 His father's job: _bus driver_

3 | Reading for detail

As its name indicates, this means reading to find out precise information about particular points.

Now read paragraph 1 again in order to answer these two questions:

1 Is Eugene already earning £35,000 a year?
   _NO_
2 Why is Eugene a 'remarkable high-flying professional'? _because he is 16-teen._

4 | Guessing the meaning of words from context

When reading something, even in your own language, you sometimes come across a word whose meaning you don't know, but you are able to work out roughly what it means because of the surrounding language. We use this skill in a lot of everyday reading when we guess what a word must mean approximately – otherwise we would be running to a dictionary all the time.

Read the relevant parts of the article again and work out what these words mean:

1 calibre (l.8) 2 launched (l.33) 3 bonuses (l.36)

standard _sength forth_ _additional awards_

5 | Inference

Often writers and speakers don't say exactly what they mean: they won't give information explicitly, but just give clues, and leave the reader or listener to deduce their real message. A politician, for example, might say: 'The unemployment figures are not exactly good', and leave his audience to *infer* that the figures are in fact rather bad. To infer means that we must learn to 'read between the lines.'

Read the article again and answer the questions below:

1 Did Eugene's parents like him studying late at night when he was younger?
2 What does the article suggest other parents might feel about a son like Eugene? } How do you know?

No they did not because he was reading under the bedclothing

They might be jelous

9

Grammar

1 Inversion constructions

Not only DOES Eugene Evans EARN a high salary, **but** he is **also** very intelligent.
Rarely HAS a 16-year-old EARNED so much money.

The two sentences above contain examples of 'inversion'. Inversions
are necessary in English when certain words are placed at the
beginning of a sentence. Their effect is to make the sentence more
dramatic or rhetorical. Compare these two:

HE NEVER WENT abroad in his whole life. v. **Never** in his whole life DID HE GO abroad.

Here is a list of some the words that must be followed by an inversion
construction when they begin a sentence. Most have a negative meaning
attached to them. Study them, then do the exercise:

Never (has she seen . . .)/**Nowhere** (will you find . . .)/**Seldom** (do you find . . .)/
Rarely (does she say . . .)/**Only then** (did I realise . . .)

Not only (did he earn . . .) **but** (he) **also** . . .
No sooner (had I entered . . .) **than** . . .
Scarcely/Hardly (had he opened . . .) **when/before** . . .

NOTE: **Only when/Not until** (something happened) (did I understand . . .)

Rephrase the following sentences beginning with the words given in brackets:

1 People rarely appreciate the full force of heredity.
   (Rarely . . .)
2 He started computer programming as soon as he
   left school. (No sooner . . .)
3 Besides earning a fortune, Eugene has also
   delighted his father. (Not only . . .)
4 We won't know how the twins feel about each other
   until they have met for the first time. (Not until . . .)
5 Such research has never been carried out before.
   (Never before . . .)
6 You seldom find reunited twins who do not get on
   well together. (Seldom . . .)
7 Eugene Evans had scarcely left school before he
   found a job in a computer software company.
   (Scarcely . . .)
8 He didn't realise how talented he was until he
   started work. (Only when . . .)
9 They had hardly been reunited when they were
   deep in conversation about the past. (Hardly . . .)
10 You won't find a school anywhere whose pupils get
   such good results. (Nowhere . . .)

2 Tenses: A reminder

Discuss these questions about the exercise above:

1 Why is the Simple Past tense used in no. 2 and the
   Present Perfect in no. 3?
2 Why is the Present Perfect tense used in no. 5?
3 In no 1, why *can't* we say 'People are rarely
   appreciating . . .'?
4 Why is the Simple Past tense used in no. 8, and not
   the Present Perfect?
5 What tenses are used in no. 7, and why?

Homework exercise   (Recommended time: 1 hour)

Plan and write a composition of about 250 words on one of the following:

1 Children today are brighter than those of previous generations. Discuss.
2 State education has lessened the effect of hereditary factors. Discuss.

TEST   **READING COMPREHENSION**   (Time: 15 minutes)

Read this passage carefully. Then choose which you think is the best suggested answer or way of finishing the statement in each item below – A, B, C or D. Write your answers on a piece of paper.

Mrs Jean Jarvis and Mrs Maureen O'Brien live a few miles apart in Essex. They are identical twins, but they were adopted at birth, and reared separately. Yet the similarities in their patterns of life, school reports, interests and family size – they both have one son and one daughter – have made them walking laboratories for scientists, who are fascinated to discover what influences hereditary factors in people.

From such research, psychologists hope to discover more about the mysteries of genetic engineering for manipulating individual genes under the microscope. Scientists still do not understand why and how an embryo developing from a single fertilised egg can separate into two identical people. Jean and Maureen are involved in these investigations as part of a project called the Minnesota Study of Twins Reared Apart, which is being undertaken by a team working with Professor Thomas Bouchard.

The pointers from that work confirm that the effect of genetic influence on intelligence is stronger (about 60 per cent to 40 per cent) than the environmental influence and that the genetic influence on personality is about 50 per cent, the other 50 per cent being influenced by environment.

The twins are participating with 28 other pairs, each reared apart, in an effort to estimate the relative contribution of genes and environment for a wide range of events during the human lifetime. These include dietary habits, the age at which specific changes in body weight occurred, age at marriage, age at birth of children, and spacing of children, age of puberty and menopause, age of starting of smoking and drinking, and so on.

Overall, a substantial genetic influence is found likely in the timing of these events. The environmental factors contributing to these behaviour patterns are more difficult to identify.

1 Scientists are primarily interested in Jean and Maureen because they

   A were adopted at birth.
   B each have a son and a daughter.
   C are identical twins who have never lived apart.
   D can help research into the influence of hereditary factors.

2 One of the aims of the Minnesota Study is to

   A discover the principles of genetic engineering.
   B help people like Jean and Maureen understand each other.
   C research the causes of human behaviour.
   D increase our information about the environment.

3 'Personality is influenced as much by genes as by the environment.' The results of the Minnesota Study so far

   A prove conclusively that this statement is true.
   B suggest that this statement is true.
   C cast considerable doubt on this statement.
   D disprove the truth of this statement.

4 From the Study of Twins Reared Apart, it would seem that

   A our dietary habits are influenced by puberty.
   B there is an important genetic contribution to the timing of many events in our lives.
   C whether we start smoking or drinking depends a great deal on intelligence.
   D the age at which we get married is determined solely by environment.

2 Generations

1 What's the gist of the following article? Read it in about five minutes to find out. What would be a good magazine headline for the article?

My son John, born 15 years ago, was my first child. He seemed to fulfil the promise of his birth – he was bright, sociable and happy. His school record was reasonable and he seemed to get on well with teachers and children alike. But when we moved to London, because of my husband's promotion, John seemed unable to settle down. Teachers complained he was anti-social and rude. He didn't make friends, and often arrived at school late and dishevelled. –(unkempt (hdung@ny))

By the time he was 12 he was steadily playing truant and in bad company. At 13, puberty struck.

He hid in his room till he was dressed, and locked the bathroom door. 'Girlie' magazines were found in his room, cigarette stubs appeared in the unlikeliest places.

Then, he started attacking the furniture and window-sills with knives or deliberately burning carpets and furniture with cigarettes, having mini bonfires in his room, and clothes and bedding were slashed.

Constant complaints

The worry and strain started then. The constant complaints from the school, the constant rows between father and son over damage. The school called me to a meeting. They could do no more, they said. He was disruptive, unruly and fostered friendships with the worst boys in the school.

When John was asked to leave the school, I began to feel despair creeping over me. I felt unable to go on, but knew I had to and as we tried to pinpoint John's problems and find something akin to a solution, I wasn't aware things could get worse. related

In disgrace

John was to be without a school for five long tedious months. He was tried at a couple of schools but they lasted, despite fervent promises on John's part, only a day or two, until he left, in disgrace.

Soon he started sleeping out, in the woods, in goods yards, waiting rooms, in a park – sharing a shed with a tramp. And often, we just never found out where.

A place was finally found for John at a 'special unit'. It proved to be warm, friendly and suited to the child's ability to progress, rather than his ability to stick to a timetable and uniform.

The teacher was warm, motherly and something of a genius with children. She liked John. The only drawback was that he could have just $2\frac{1}{2}$ days at the unit. He enjoyed it, but the rest of the time was empty and heavy for him.

Forebodings

For a time John stopped sleeping out, but the destruction continued. His behaviour and manner improved, he began to take an interest in his appearance. We spent a lot of time together and talked. He co-operated with his social workers.

I held my breath. Had the 'phase' finally passed? Things seemed to be going well.

Two things then happened which foreboded things to come. John and his friend got into our back garden, where the garage was, and John, boasting of a driving prowess he didn't possess, started the car (accidentally in reverse) and went through the back of the garage the hard way.

More serious was his theft of our holiday savings – £60. The money had been carefully hidden in the sideboard.

But a new cycle had begun, because with the disappearance of the money, came the disappearance of our son. For ten days.

Glue sniffing

Eventually he returned. But he was different. He had met skinheads. He knew more than when he left. He had been 'sniffing'. Glue held the keys of paradise.

John started coming in late, if at all. More than once on bitterly cold winter mornings I would find him cold, stiff and asleep on our patio. No explanations for his absences. Red nosed and pimply from the glue, sores around the mouth, smells on his clothes.

He began to talk with a coarse Cockney accent, deliberately ungrammatical, presumably to hide his origins from other skinheads.

Then John was caught shoplifting, twice, and he was charged.

Conditional discharge

After long and involved reports he was given a conditional discharge, lasting a year. John had seemed shaken by the formality of the court. He promised as we walked to the car that he would behave in future.

Then he began to sniff glue in the house. On my return the house would stink of some substance or there would be an overwhelming smell of airfreshener.

The burning of furniture, other damage and the stealing all began again and escalated. He held on to reality by a thread, and it became more and more apparent to me that whatever he was on —whether exclusively glue or worse—it was attacking his mind more savagely than any 'teenage phase' could account for.

Finally he went 'walkabout' for three weeks. My husband, at the end of his wits, felt the best thing would be if John were in care. I couldn't agree but I couldn't think what else to do either.

Sense of betrayal
No-one can know the sense of betrayal I felt when John phoned and I asked him to stay where he was. Instead of setting out for him on that cold bleak night I phoned the police and emergency social worker who got a magistrate up to sign the order for John to be placed in care.

He is in care until he is 18.

The worst thing is the loss of love and trust. The desolation and heartbreak is indescribable and the son who was warm and happy, mischievous and settled, died a long time ago just as surely as a boy run over by a bus.

---

2 Are the following statements true or false? Give reasons.

1 John was an only child. *F*
2 John annoyed one teacher in particular. *F*
3 John missed a lot of schooling. *T*
4 The special unit had a rigid timetable. *F*
5 John's behaviour grew steadily worse, without any change, from the age of thirteen. *T*

3 Write down at least four adjectives to describe

1 John's attitude to school, society or authority; and
2 his parents' attitude towards him.

Compare your lists with a partner's.

1) antisocial, rude, disruptive, unruly
2) understanding, tolerant, patient, forgiving

4 Complete the blanks in the following sentences:

1 He was said to have shared a shed with a _tramp_.
2 John was only allowed to spend __2½__ days at the unit.
3 John drove the car through the __back__ of the garage.
4 The family had saved __£60__ for their holiday.
5 John started to speak with a _Cockney_ accent.

5 What reading skills have you employed in exercises 1–4?

6 Discussion
What do you think of the parents' decision to put John 'in care'? Do you approve or disapprove? Why? *I approve because the parents have tried so many times and it didn't seem to help, and John's condition, mental & physical, started to be hopeless. Only the unit care could help him.*

Grammar
Verb + noun/pronoun/possessive adjective + gerund

John hated his mother (*or* his mother's) complaining about the way he spoke.
The teachers couldn't understand John (*or* John's) disrupting the class.
John's parents couldn't get used to him (*or* his) staying away from home.

This common English construction often occurs with verbs that express an attitude towards other people's actions or beliefs.

1 Study this table and make complete sentences from it:

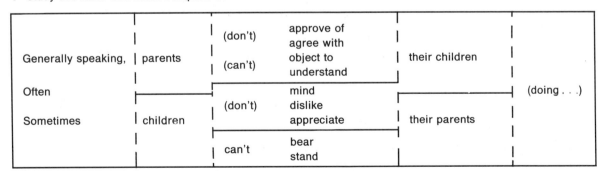

Generally speaking,	parents	(don't)	approve of agree with object to understand	their children	(doing . . .)
Often			mind		
Sometimes	children	(don't)	dislike appreciate	their parents	
		can't	bear stand		

2 Make sentences (in the present and past) about yourself and classmates with the same verbs:

My . . .'s parents . . . . my/me his/him/her . . . . ing . . . . .

3 Make a list of things you approve or disapprove of other people doing, then discuss them.

The discursive composition

In the Proficiency Paper 2 (Composition) there is nearly always a discursive composition title, i.e. one which asks you to give your opinion on or outline the arguments for and against a particular issue or point of view. The following are examples of discursive composition titles:

– Outline the advantages and disadvantages of having children.
– It is the duty of parents to look after their children in whatever circumstances.
– Children should be guided and corrected, but never punished. Discuss.

1 How to approach a discursive composition

1 *Always read the composition title very carefully.* This may seem obvious, but it is very important that your composition should be 100% relevant to the title. Notice particularly whether the title asks you to give your opinion or merely to outline general arguments. Notice too the number of words expected: a phrase such as 'about 300 words' is often used in the Proficiency Paper.

What do the composition titles above ask for – your opinion, or arguments?

2 *Plan your composition.* That is, before you start to write the composition –
a) write notes of the main points you wish to make;
b) work out what order you wish to put these points in;
c) divide your points into paragraphs.

A typical plan for the first composition above ('Outline the advantages and disadvantages of having children.') might be as follows:

Paragraph 1: General introduction to theme
Paragraph 2: Advantages : - security in old age
                          - companionship
                          - pleasure in creating and raising life
                          - help to strengthen a marriage
                          - prevent couples becoming too selfish
Paragraph 3: Disadvantages: - expensive
                          - risky; children may turn out 'badly'
                          - time- consuming; stop you doing other things
                          - difficult to combine. with career(s)
Paragraph 4: Conclusion: weigh advantages against disadvantages, with own opinion

REMEMBER:
a) A plan is just a note or reminder to yourself, so it only needs to include the main points which you will then expand upon in the composition itself.
b) The contents of the plan must only reflect your opinion if the title asks for it.
c) When you are required to give your point of view, remember to justify and explain it.
d) The plan above follows a basic discursive composition pattern:

INTRODUCTION → DEVELOPMENT → CONCLUSION

Although this may not fit every composition or may not always suit your own personal style of writing, it provides a very useful outline for a discursive composition.

3 *Write the composition.* When you have planned your composition carefully, write it, remembering to connect the points in your plan well. Here is some useful language for doing this.

For listing arguments or points

First / Firstly / First of all
Second / Secondly / Next
Third / Thirdly / Next
etc.
Finally / Lastly / Last of all

For exemplifying

For example / For instance / e.g.
To take (just) one example, . . .
A clear example of . . . is/might be . . .

For rephrasing

In other words / To be precise /
That is to say

For concluding

In brief / In short / In conclusion
To conclude / To summarise

Other generally useful phrases

In my opinion, . . . / To my mind . . .
As far as X is concerned / As for X / As regards X / Regarding X, . . .
Generally speaking, . . .
It is often claimed/argued/said/thought etc. that . . .
It is undeniable that . . . / There can be no doubt that . . .

4 *Check it.* When you have written your composition, check it very carefully – and make sure you always give yourself time to check it – looking at the following:

– Grammar
– Spelling
– Punctuation
– Vocabulary

All students tend to make their own particular mistakes, so it is useful for you to establish exactly what your weaknesses are, and then to watch out for them and correct them when they occur. (See also Unit 12.)

– Relevance   Everything in the composition must be relevant to the title.
– Style   Unit 7 in this course deals more with style.
– Length   The composition must be the length required in the instructions.

2 Exercises in composition planning

1 Write a plan for this composition:
'It is the duty of parents to look after their children in whatever circumstances.'
Allow yourself 10 minutes only.

2 In pairs examine your composition plans together and decide:
a) Are all the contents relevant?
b) Are the plans sufficiently comprehensive, or too full or incomplete?
c) Are the plans well ordered?

3 In pairs, write a plan for this composition:
'Children should be guided and corrected, but never punished.'
Discuss the issues among yourselves before writing the plan.

4 For homework, write the composition 'Outline the advantages and disadvantages of having children'. Follow the plan on page 14 (opposite) if you wish and try to write the composition in an hour.

Listening

'Substitute Parents'

1 Before you listen, say what you remember about
John (pp.12–13).
Why do you think John behaved as he did?
What could the following have done to help him, to
prevent him from sliding into bad company,
stealing and glue-sniffing:
a) his parents? b) his teachers?
c) social workers? d) society?

 2 You are going to hear an interview with a
sociologist. Listen to find out his general views
about the family today and about substitute
parents.

 3 Now listen again and make notes on the following
points (on a piece of paper):

1 What people have been saying for years about 'the
family and family life': _____

2 What Dr Neil said about
a) divorce: _____
b) re-marriage: _____
c) single-parent families: _____
d) 'dual career' families: _____

3 The views of many listeners on 'dual career'
families: _____

4 The different 'substitute parents' mentioned are
(*list*): _____

5 Why it is said the mixing of ages is important: ____

4 Discussion

To what extent do you think family life today accounts for 'problem
children' like John? And what about city life? Do you think John would
have gone off the rails if the family had not moved to London?

Vocabulary

More words for joining sentences

A variety of joining words makes for a far more interesting style of writing
and allows for more precise expression. Study and do these exercises.

1 Words that introduce contrasting information: *whereas*, *though*, *despite*, etc.

> He promised he would behave **but** in fact he quickly went back to his old ways.

Rephrase this sentence using the words in the sentences below. Be careful!
You may have to make changes in punctuation or in grammatical construction,
or both.

1 Whereas _he promised to behave, he quickly went to his old way_
2 On the one hand _he promised to behave on the other hand_
3 Much though _____
4 _____. However, _____

5 Despite *he's promising to behave*

6 .... Nevertheless, ...

7 In spite of the fact that *he promised to behave*

8 Although ....

9 While ....

10 .... yet ....

Do you know any other 'contrast' words? Make a list of them.
What grammatical constructions do they require?

2 Words that introduce additional information: *besides, moreover, too*, etc.

> John had met some skinheads **and** he had been sniffing glue.

Rephrase this sentence using the words below.

1 Not only .... but ....

2 In addition to ....

3 .... Moreover, ...

4 Besides ....

5 .... What's more, ...

What other 'addition' words do you know? Make a list of them.
What grammatical constructions do they require?

3 Style Some of the joining words in **1** and **2** are more appropriate to certain styles of writing than others. Go through the sentences you have written again and put a letter beside each to indicate the style or register: 'N' for Neutral and 'F' for Formal.

Homework exercises   (Recommended time: 40 minutes)

Write plans for the three following discursive composition titles.

1 A child is influenced as much by his schooling as by his parents. Discuss.

2 The generation gap is the result of a lack of communication between parents and their children. Discuss.

3 All young people going on to higher education should be obliged to go out to work for a year before doing so. Discuss the pros and cons of such a proposal.

TEST   **COMPOSITION**   (Time: 1 hour)

Write one only *of the following composition exercises. Your answers must follow exactly the instructions given.*

1 It's the duty of parents to look after their children in whatever circumstances. Discuss. (About 300 words)

2 Parents learn as much from their children as children learn from their parents – at least they should do. Give your opinion. (About 300 words)

3 Mysteries and Theories

[handwritten: UFO – unidentified flying objects.]

1 You have probably heard or read about many unexplained mysteries such as the 'Mary Celeste', the Bermuda Triangle, UFOs, the Abominable Snowman (in the Himalayas), the Loch Ness Monster (in Scotland), the 'Curse of the Pharaohs', and why and how the Pyramids were built in Egypt.

Tell each other briefly what you know about any of these 'mysteries', and also any of the theories which have been put forward to explain them.

[handwritten: ragi antlers]

2 Now read this and do the exercise below.

[handwritten: incinerating – burning, foliage – leaves]

THE SIBERIAN MYSTERY

At 7.17 a.m., local time, on 30 June 1908 a fireball of devastating proportions struck Earth in the valley of the Tunguska river, a remote part of northern Siberia. Its blazing heat flattened an area the size of Leningrad, melting metal objects and incinerating herds of reindeer. Foliage was ripped from trees, the blast uprooting them like matchsticks. Nomads were lifted bodily from the ground and their tents flung away in the violent wind. A farmer sitting on his porch 60 kilometres away described it: 'There appeared a great flash of light. There was so much heat that I was no longer able to remain where I was – my shirt almost burned off my back. I saw a huge fireball that covered an enormous part of the sky. I only had a moment to note the size of it. Afterwards it became dark and at the same time I felt an explosion that threw me several feet from the porch. I lost consciousness for a few moments and when I came to, I heard a noise that shook the whole house and nearly moved it off its foundations.'

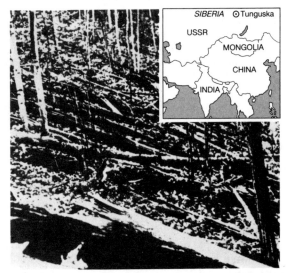

Various theories

Whatever caused the Tunguska explosion, it wasn't a meteorite, it seems.

The controversy about possible causes has split investigators into those who believe that it was a comet (a kind of dirty cosmic snowball consisting of chunks of frozen gases with meteoritic material and dust mixed in), and those who prefer a more fanciful explanation.

Findings from many sources now strongly favour the comet, but the last word has certainly not been said.

The alternative theories are in any case provocative and appealing enough to be worth considering.

[handwritten: it doesn't mean that this is comet]

According to what you have read, are these statements true or false? Give reasons.

1 The area which was hit was quite densely populated. *F*
2 The heat was so intense that it burned or melted almost everything in the area. *T*
3 The light lit up a huge area for hours. *F*

4 Investigators fall into two categories: those who believe a meteorite caused the explosion, and those who favour some other explanation. *F*
5 One of the theories suggests that the area was hit by a comet. *T*

1) Comets can change direction
vet speed & they have
their temp.
2) If the comete hit the
earth it would
produce nuclear effects
3) Cometes which come
from a point in the
dawn shy close to
the sun are difficult
to detect and observe.

3 Jigsaw reading

1 Break into small groups. Each group should read two of the theories
below only (Theories 1 and 2, or Theories 3 and 4) and take notes on
the main points of each Theory together with any objections to it. All
group members should take notes for themselves.
2 Then, working from your notes, find out from another student what the
other theories were and the objections to them.
3 Discuss which theory you think best accounts for the Siberian Mystery.

The Theories

1 Black holes

Although as yet unproved, there is strong theoretical
support for the idea that after the creation of our universe a
number of 'black holes' were left. A 'black hole' is an area in
outer space into which everything near it, including light
itself is pulled. The theory is that if a body is reduced to a
black hole, it becomes extremely small and dense. According to the British physicists A.A. Jackson and M.P. Ryan in
Nature, the effect of a black hole hitting Siberia would be
indistinguishable from the Tunguska event. Another scientist states that an 'atom-sized black hole entering the Earth's
atmosphere at a typical collision velocity for an interplan-
etary body would create an atmospheric shock wave with
enough force to level hundreds of square kilometres of
Siberian forest, and produce flash-burning and seismic
effects. The black hole would then follow a rather straight
path through the body of the Earth with very little
interaction and emerge a few minutes later on the opposite
side of the Earth.'

Since the theory was propounded, the objections have
been made that there is no record of an unusual explosion
on that day in the North Atlantic where it would have
emerged from Earth, and further that a black hole would
cause very severe subterranean shock waves, whereas the
only recorded seismic effects were surface waves.

2 Anti-matter

Anti-matter is matter or material made up of negative
particles with an existence predicted on the basis of the
relativity theory and quantum mechanics. Research into
anti-matter is still in its infancy, but one theory suggests that
the Earth was hit by an 'anti-matter meteorite'. As far as
Tunguska is concerned, however, it seems an unlikely
solution since 'anti-matter meteorites' are supposed to
originate far beyond the Milky Way and would lose their
explosive power by the time they reached our galaxy.
Nevertheless, several renowned scientists prefer this as an
explanation.

3 Extra-terrestrial nuclear explosion

The idea of Earth being hit by a nuclear explosion was first
put forward in a science fiction work in 1946 by the Russian,
Alexander Kazantsev, who was convinced the Tunguska
explosion was the result of a nuclear explosion in a space
ship. This would explain the radial scorching and the
undamaged trees at the centre, the descriptions of a pillar of
fire and billowing dust cloud consistent with the now-
familiar mushroom cloud of an atomic explosion, why there
was no crater, and why the object – whatever it was –
appeared to slow down as it neared Earth. Other writers
have suggested that it was a space ship powered by anti-
matter that exploded after getting into trouble.

4 The comet hypothesis

This would seem to be the best explanation. Comets have
been known to change direction and speed. In 1977 it was
calculated that although the temperature produced by a
comet in the atmosphere would have been no more than a
few million degrees, it could well have produced nuclear
effects if it hit the Earth. As to why the comet (if that is what it
was) was not observed for a longer time, the following
explanation has been given: 'When the comet encountered
the Earth, it would be coming from a point in the dawn sky
comparatively close to the Sun and would thus be most
difficult to detect and observe.'

Summary writing

1 In Section B of the Proficiency Paper 3 (Use of English) you will be asked to write a summary. Imagine you are asked to 'summarise and compare the first two theories put forward to account for the mysterious event in Tunguska in 1908'. Read the first two theories on page 19 again, and study the main points and summary below. Note the connectors that have been used (and see Unit 2, pp.16–17 for others).

Summary

Two of the theories which have been propounded to explain the Tunguska explosion are the 'black hole' theory and the 'anti-matter' theory. *While* it is as yet unproved that a black hole or anti-matter caused the explosion, there is theoretical scientific support for their existence.

A 'black hole' is believed to be extremely dense *and* the effect of one hitting the Earth would produce the same effect as that in Tunguska. It would create a massive shock wave *which* would flatten and burn large areas of forest. *Furthermore*, it would pass through the Earth and out the other side, *yet* there was no evidence of any Atlantic explosion nor of any subterranean earthquakes in the Tunguska incident.

The anti-matter theory *also* seems to give an unlikely explanation of the mystery. Anti-matter meteorites are supposed to come from beyond the Milky Way, *and* would *therefore* lose much of their explosive power if they reached Earth. *Nevertheless*, research into anti-matter is still young, *and* this explanation is preferred by some scientists.

Main points

1 a) Not yet proved – strong theoretical support for idea of 'black holes'.
 b) 'Black hole' – very dense.
 c) Effect of an atom-size 'black hole' hitting Siberia – same as Tunguska event.
 d) Would create massive shock wave – flatten large area of forest – other effects.
 e) Black hole would pass through Earth and out other side. No evidence: no Atlantic explosion: no subterranean earthquakes.
2 a) Anti-matter: again only theory.
 b) Anti-matter meteorites supposed to come from beyond the Milky Way – lose power on reaching Earth.
 c) BUT research into anti-matter still young – this explanation preferred by some scientists.

2 How to approach writing a summary

1 Pick out the part or parts of the text that must be summarised. Often you will not have to summarise a whole text.
2 Read the part or parts of the text for gist. Ask yourself what it is/they are about.
3 Underline or circle the main points (words, phrases or sentences).
4 Make a list of the main points i.e. write them down.
5 Re-order or re-group the points as appropriate.
6 Decide which points need to be linked with which joining words.
7 Write your summary.
8 Read it carefully, correcting where necessary, and check the number of words.

3 Now summarise and compare the final two theories (Theories 3 and 4 on page 19) put forward to account for the mysterious event in Tunguska in 1908. Work in pairs for steps 1–6 in **2**.

Grammar

The use or absence of the definite article *the*

1

1 Remember that *the* defines particular things, but is not used when we want to talk about things in general, for example:

This is a novel of *nations* at *war*.
The nations that were involved in *the 1914–18 war* all suffered dreadfully.

2 *The* is not usually used with . . .
Stars/planets: Sirius; Mars, Jupiter
Continents: Europe, Africa, Antarctica
(BUT the Antarctic, the Arctic)
States/Counties: Texas, Siberia, Kent
Countries: Portugal, Italy, England
(BUT the USA, the USSR)
Cities/Towns: Bonn, London, New York
Mountains: Mount Everest
Lakes: Lake Como, Loch Ness
Streets: Oxford Street, London Road
Magazines: 'Life', 'Time', 'Nature'
Buildings: York Minster, Gatwick Airport

The is usually used with . . .
the Universe, the Milky Way
The solar system: the Sun, the Moon, the Earth
Areas: the Middle East
Seas/Oceans: the Atlantic, the Black Sea
Island groups: the British Isles
Mountain chains: the Himalayas
Rivers: the Nile, the Tunguska
Deserts: the Kalahari, the Sahara
Hotels: the Dorchester (Hotel)
Cinemas/Theatres: the Odeon, the Galaxy
Newspapers: 'The Times', 'The Express'

3 *The* is not usually used with *names of people* or with *'titles'* e.g. John Smith, Dr Smith, Lord and Lady Smith, Captain Smith, or with 'personification' e.g. Mother Earth.

BUT NOTE the use of *the* in e.g.
'That's the Captain Smith I told you about'; and
'Her name's Margaret Thatcher.'
'You mean – *the* Margaret Thatcher?!'

4 *The* is not usually used with *days of the week*, *months*, *festivals* (e.g. Christmas Day) *or seasons*, except when specifying, e.g.

Do you remember the winter of 1975?
The Saturday we moved into our new house was awful!
I remember the Christmas Day we received the news.

2 Put in *the* or nothing, as appropriate, in this piece of science fiction.

We came screaming in towards _the_ solar system from _the_ outer reaches of _the_ Milky Way. We had been away a long time, a very long time, but we calculated that down on ___ Earth it was ___ Easter Sunday, 2095. _The_ Sun, our very own sun, was in view: then on through _the_ system past ___ Neptune, ___ Jupiter, ___ Mars and ___ other planets until _the_ Earth and _the_ Moon came clearly into view on our screens. There was ___ silence in _the_ ship, each crew member with his or her own thoughts. And as we drew nearer and prepared to orbit ___ Mother Earth, we could make out _the_ Atlantic, _the_ Arctic and _the_ continents of ___ Europe and ___ Asia. Nearer still, and we could clearly distinguish other familiar features – _the_ Himalayas, _the_ Mediterranean Sea and _the_ Nile, _the_ British Isles, ___ Italy and _the_ Iberian Peninsula. And I imagined _the_ people in ___ Scandinavia, ___ Africa and _the_ USSR watching for our return. Yet as we drew nearer still, features in detail were not so familiar, and I had a dread of what we might find.

Listening

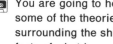

You are going to hear a brief radio interview in which an author explains some of the theories put forward to account for the famous sea mystery surrounding the ship the 'Mary Celeste'. Listen and make notes on the facts of what happened and on the different theories. Then compare your notes with your partner's.

Reading and filling in blanks

1 In Section A of the Proficiency Paper 3 (Use of English) you will be asked to read a passage and fill in the blanks. If you were given a piece of writing in your own language which had blanks or gaps in it, you would probably be able to read it. Why? Because you know the systems in your own language well enough to be able to guess what is missing. You can do this in English, too. But here are some tips to help you.

1 Read the whole text or paragraph through to get the gist of it.

2 Then go back, read each sentence with a blank in it carefully, and ask yourself this question: What kind of word is needed in the blank – an adjective? a verb? a joining word? a modal (e.g. *should*) or an auxiliary verb (e.g. *have*, *be*)? a word like *a*, *the*, *some*, *few*, etc.? The words before and after the blank will give you clues.

3 Then, when you think you know what kind of word is missing and what is required for meaning, check different words to see how and if they will fit. For example, if you are sure a preposition is missing, is it to do with time (*at, on, in, for, since, ago*, etc.), with location (*at, under, near*, etc.) or with movement (*to, by, past, into*, etc.)? Or is it part of a set Noun/Verb/Adjective + Preposition phrase (*in the absence of, rely on, proud of*, etc.)? Or if it is a joining word, could it be *although, and, which/that/who, besides*, etc., or part of a phrase, such as *as* in *as good as*, or *so* in *so relieved that*, etc.?

2 Read the passage below. Then fill in the blanks, asking yourself the questions above and questions like those down the right-hand column below. Check your completions with a partner.

Is there any logical explanation __of__ (1) the mysterious deaths of __so__ (2) many people? Journalist Phillip Vendenberg studied the legend of the Curse of the Pharaohs for years. He came __up__ (3) with a fascinating suggestion. In his book, 'The Curse of the Pharaohs', he says that the tombs within the Pyramids were perfect breeding grounds for bacteria __which__ (4) could develop new and unknown strains __over__ (5) the centuries and could maintain their potency until the present day.

He also points __out__ (6) that the ancient Egyptians were experts in poison. Some poisons do not have to be swallowed to kill – they can prove lethal __often__ (7) penetrating the skin. Poisonous substances were used in wall paintings within the tombs, which were __often__ (8) sealed and made airtight. Grave-robbers __who__ (9) in ancient days raided the tombs always first bored a small hole __in__ (10) the chamber wall to allow __the__ (11) air to circulate before they broke __through__ (12) to plunder the Pharaohs' riches.

But the __most__ (13) extraordinary explanation _____ (14) all for the Curse was put __forward__ (15) in 1949. It came from the atomic scientist Professor Louis Bulgarini. He said: 'It is definitely possible that __the__ (16) ancient Egyptians used atomic radiation to __secure__ (17) their holy places. The floors of the tombs __must__ (18) have been finished with radio-active rock. Rock containing __the__ (19) gold and uranium was mined in Egypt 3,000 years ago. __This__ (20) radiation could kill a man today.

1 Preposition! *of*? *about*? *to* as in *explain something to somebody*? *for*?

2 What words can go in front of *many*? *too, not, so*? How about *such*?

3 Phrasal verb! *in*? *down*? *through*? *by*? *up*? *to*?

4 Read the whole sentence. The missing word *must* join the two! *and*? *but*? *which*? *that*? *who*?

5 Time preposition! *during*? *over*? *through(out)*?

6 Phrasal verb! *to*? *out*? *up*?

7 Must mean: *when they penetrate . . .* So *on* or *by*? Or perhaps *after*?

8 Surely a time word of some kind: *often*? *then*? *sometimes*? *always*?

9 Read the whole sentence. Must be a relative pronoun: *that*? *which*? *who*?

10 Preposition! *round*? *through*? *in*? *across*?

Homework exercise   (Recommended time: 30 minutes)

Summary

Read the completed passage above again and then summarise in about 70 words the theories which have been propounded to explain why so many people connected with the discovery of Tutankhamun have died from the 'Curse of the Pharaohs'.

TEST　　　　　　　**USE OF ENGLISH**　　　　　(Time: 45 minutes)

1 *Fill each of the numbered blanks in the following passage with* one *suitable word.*

If there is ___a___(1) truth ___in___(2) the belief that the ancient Pharaohs can be ___made___(3) responsible ___for___(4) 20th-century deaths, ___then___(5) there is one case ___which___(6) overshadows all others. ___In___(7) 1912, a liner was crossing ___the___(8) Atlantic with a valuable cargo – an Egyptian mummy. ___It___(9) was the body of a prophetess who lived ___in___(10) the reign of Tutankhamun's father-in-law, Akhenaton, An ornament found ___on___(11) the mummy bore a spell: 'Awake ___from___(12) the dream in which you sleep and you will triumph over all that is done against you.' ___Because___(13) of its value, the mummy ___was___(14) not carried in the liner's hold, ___but___(15) in a compartment behind the bridge on ___which___(16) stood the captain, ___some___(17) errors of judgment played a part in ___causing___(18) his ship to sink. The story of the sinking of ___the___(19) ship, and of the death of 1,513 passengers aboard her, has been ___known___(20) elsewhere. Her name was the *Titanic*.

2　Read this passage carefully, then in about 80 words summarise how Father Brown tested his suspicions about Flambeau and what his subsequent course of action was.

'I'm afraid I watched you, you know,' said Father Brown to Flambeau. 'So at last I saw you change the parcels. Then, don't you see, I changed them back again, and then I left the right one behind.'

'Left it behind?' repeated Flambeau, shifting uneasily in his priestly disguise.

'Well, it was like this,' said the little priest, speaking in the same unaffected way. 'I went back to that sweet-shop and asked if I'd left a parcel, and gave them a particular address if it turned up. Well, I knew I hadn't; but when I went away again I did. So, instead of running after me with that valuable parcel, they have sent it flying to a friend of mine in Westminster.' Then he added rather sadly: 'I learnt that, too, from a poor fellow in Hartlepool. He used to do it with handbags he stole at railway stations.'

Flambeau tore a brown-paper parcel out of his inner pocket and rent it in pieces. Instead of the cross, there was nothing but paper and sticks of lead inside it. He sprang to his feet with a gigantic gesture, and cried: 'I don't believe you. I don't believe an idiot like you could manage all that. I believe you've still got the stuff on you, and if you don't give it up – why, we're all alone, and I'll take it by force!'

'No,' said Father Brown simply, and stood up also; 'you won't take it by force. First, because I really haven't got it. And, second, because we are not alone.'

Flambeau stopped in his stride forward. 'Behind that tree,' said Father Brown, pointing, 'are two strong policemen and the greatest detective alive. How did they come here, do you ask? Why, I brought them, of course! How did I do it? Well, I wasn't sure you were a thief, and it would never do to make a scandal against one of our own clergy. So I just tested you to see if anything would make you show yourself. A man generally makes a scene if he finds salt in his coffee; if he doesn't, he has some reason for keeping quiet. I changed the salt and sugar and *you* kept quiet. A man generally objects if his bill is three times too big. If he pays, he has some motive for passing unnoticed. I altered your bill, and *you* paid it.'

The world seemed waiting for Flambeau to leap like a tiger. But he was held back by a spell; he was stunned with the utmost curiosity. 'Well,' went on Father Brown, 'as you wouldn't leave any tracks for the police, of course somebody had to. At every place we went to, I took care to do something that would get us talked about for the rest of the day. I didn't do much harm – a splashed wall, spilt apples, a broken window; but I saved the cross. It is at Westminster now.'

4 Crime and Punishment

PAPER 4: LISTENING COMPREHENSION

1 Disturbing though it must be for the population, the authorities and the police, crime in many countries, and particularly in large cities, is on the increase. As a class, briefly discuss crime in your country. For example, is crime increasing, or not? If it is, what kinds of crimes are becoming more common? And can you suggest why?

2 Preparing to listen

Three of the skills you must acquire in Listening Comprehension are

1 understanding English in a variety of 'non-standard' accents;
2 reading and interpreting graphical material (e.g. a chart); and
3 trying to predict what you are going to hear.

1 a) English is spoken by millions of people in many countries throughout the world as their native or 'first' language, and there are many quite distinct accents.

This is part of a report of an armed robbery. Study it and then listen to the way it is read by speakers with the accents listed below.

> 13th February. 9.30. 45, Green Lane, London. A Security van collecting money from the National Bank was approached by two men, one with a .45 revolver, the other with a sawn-off shotgun. When the guard was threatened with the handgun, he handed over four cash bags. Then the robbers escaped in a stolen car.

1 Australian   2 American   3 Scottish   4 Caribbean   5 Irish   6 South African   7 Welsh

b) Now you are going to hear parts of a newspaper article read with different accents. As you listen, write in the number of the speaker in the table below.

South African ☐   American ☐   Scottish ☐   Irish ☐
Welsh ☐   Caribbean ☐   Australian ☐

Compare you answers with a partner. Discuss which accent(s) you found difficult or easy to understand. Can you say why?

2 a) You are going to hear someone talking about the rise in crime. But *before you listen*, study the graphical material (right), and answer and discuss these questions:
1 What does the title tell you – 'A Decade of Crime in the Capital'?
2 What do you think is missing from boxes 1 and 3? (Can you already guess *roughly* what the answers are?)
3 What do you think is missing from boxes 2 and 4? Why?

b) Now listen and follow the instructions. Then discuss how close your predictions were.

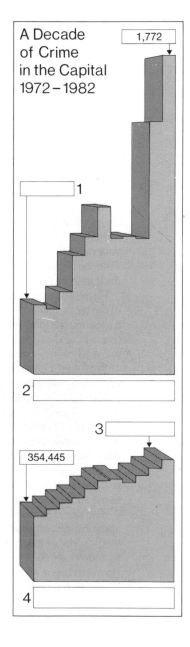

A Decade of Crime in the Capital 1972–1982

1,772

1

2

3

354,445

4

3 Listening

1 Before you listen to the tape, study the chart below and answer these
  questions:

  – Where do you think the chart is taken from? Why?
  – Do you think you are going to hear a monologue, a dialogue or a
    discussion? Why?
  – Do you understand all the crimes in the list? If not, do you think that
    the speaker or speakers will help you somehow? How?

2 Now listen and follow the instructions on the tape.

'I am going to read out a list of crimes
and for each one I would like you to tell me
which of the sentences on the card you feel
should represent the <u>maximum</u> sentence
imposed by the courts.'

	Death penalty	Life sentence	11 years to life	6-10 years	2-5 years	Under 2 years	No sentence	Don't know
Bigamy								
Blackmail								
Possession of drugs								
Hijacking								
Kidnapping								
Murder								
Armed robbery								
Theft (incl. shoplifting)								
Rape and other sexual offences								
Mugging								

3 Now compare your answers with a partner. Which do you agree with
  most – 'M' or 'W'? Why?

4 Now use the chart to conduct surveys in groups of five or six. Then one
  of each group reports to the rest of the class.

Grammar

Some adjective and adverb constructions

1 You remember that comparative adjectives are formed with adj.-*er* or *more/less*+ adj., or are irregular e.g. *better*, *worse*, *further*, etc. In the same way, comparative adverbs are formed with *more/less*+ adv., or are irregular e.g. *better*, *worse*, etc. Comparative adjectives and adverbs can be intensified by 'doubling up' e.g.

Adj.:
bigger and bigger, shorter and shorter, worse and worse, better and better

more and more	} {	common, difficult,
less and less		disturbing

Adv.:
more and more	} {	slowly, carefully,
less and less		responsibly

better and better, worse and worse, further and further, harder and harder

Now study the criminal statistics for England and Wales 1977 and 1981 and make statements about them like this:

Fraud has become less and less common in recent years.
Burglaries have become more and more frequent since 1977.

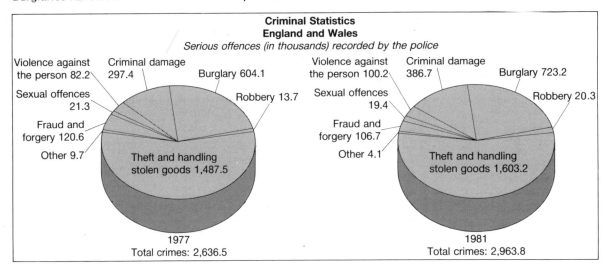

Criminal Statistics
England and Wales
Serious offences (in thousands) recorded by the police

Violence against the person 82.2
Criminal damage 297.4
Burglary 604.1
Sexual offences 21.3
Robbery 13.7
Fraud and forgery 120.6
Other 9.7
Theft and handling stolen goods 1,487.5
1977
Total crimes: 2,636.5

Violence against the person 100.2
Criminal damage 386.7
Burglary 723.2
Sexual offences 19.4
Robbery 20.3
Fraud and forgery 106.7
Other 4.1
Theft and handling stolen goods 1,603.2
1981
Total crimes: 2,963.8

2 Look at these sentences which use *the*+ comparative adj./adv., then do the exercise.

The bigger cities become, the more crime increases.	= As cities become bigger, crime increases correspondingly.
The older he gets, the less honest he becomes.	= As he gets older, he becomes correspondingly less honest.
The sooner we can solve the problem, the better it will be for all concerned.	= If we can solve the problem soon, it will be better for all concerned.

And note these two common sayings:

The sooner, the better! = The sooner something is done, the better it will be.
The more, the merrier! = The more people there are, the merrier the group will be.

Finish each of the following sentences in such a way that it means exactly
the same as the sentence printed before it.

1 As unemployment increases, crime is likely to increase too. (The more . . .)
2 If you work harder, you'll earn more money. (The harder . . .)
3 As our cities grow bigger, they become less safe. (The bigger . . .)
4 If you practise more, you'll be better. (The more . . .)
5 If we wait any longer, the situation will become more disturbing. (The longer . . .)

3 Look at these inversion constructions with adjectives and adverbs, and
then make similar statements about crime and punishment:

1
Sad as/though it is/it may be. robbery is definitely on the increase. Strange as/though it may seem, cases of fraud and forgery have decreased in number.

= Although it is/may be sad, robbery is definitely on
   the increase.
= Although it may seem strange, cases of fraud and
   forgery have decreased in number.

2
So sharp is the increase in violence So sharply have crime figures risen } that something/must be done about it.

= The increase in violence is so sharp/
   Crime figures have risen so sharply
   that something must be done about it.

Vocabulary

Describing people's reactions (with adverb-adjective collocations)

In the taped interviews earlier in the Unit (p.25), the man and the woman
used expressions like *absolutely disgusted*, *deeply disturbed* and *absolutely
amazed*. What were they referring to when they used these expressions?

You are going to hear ten people expressing their reactions to or feelings
about certain things, events, situations, etc. Below are some common
adverb-adjective collocations. Study them and then listen to the tape. As
you listen, choose and write down a phrase (e.g. *absolutely disgusted*)
which you think best describes how the speaker sounds. Then discuss
what you have written with a partner.
(Note that many of these collocations, particularly with adverbs like
deeply, *greatly*, *highly*, *thoroughly* and *utterly* are quite formal and tend to
be used in written English.)

absolutely	amazed, astonished, determined, disgusted
bitterly	disappointed
completely	bored, exhausted, overcome
deeply	depressed, disappointed, disturbed, hurt, moved, offended
extremely	annoyed
greatly	relieved
highly	amused
thoroughly	annoyed, determined, exhausted, upset
utterly	bored, depressed, disgusted
very	amused, annoyed, bored, depressed, determined, disappointed, disturbed, exhausted, relieved, upset

If you must be
depressed, why
can't you enjoy
it more?

Remember that these combinations can also be used with the *-ing*
adjective, e.g. *The film was utterly boring.*

Homework exercises

1 Summary   (Recommended time: 40 minutes)

This is an extract from a book about the history of smuggling and smugglers in the South of England. Read it carefully and then summarise in about 120 words what it says about the incidence of smuggling, the sentences given to smugglers and their attitude to imprisonment in the late 18th and early 19th centuries.

In the early 1800s smuggling gangs were generally smaller and fewer in number than they had been during the previous century, they were operating less frequently, and the amount of contraband arriving in Dorset was greatly reduced. Furthermore the number of runs being intercepted and the number of smugglers arrested had increased dramatically. There is clear evidence for this in the registers of Dorchester Gaol, which survive from 1782. In the thirty-three years from then to 1815, just sixty-two smugglers were imprisoned at Dorchester – an average of less than two a year; in the following thirty-three years, from 1816 to 1848, the number totalled 749 – an average of twenty-three a year. And if the five years beginning 1821 are taken in isolation, the average annual figure rises to forty-eight, prompting the Clerk of the Peace for Dorset to remark in 1825 that the ratio of smugglers to other offenders in the prison was 'a constant subject of regret to the visiting Justices'.

In the same report, the clerk stated there had been few instances of insubordination or discontent in the prison and the general demeanour of the prisoners had been regular and orderly, 'the only particular exception having taken place in the smuggling wards'. Similarly, the prison chaplain reported that the spiritual condition of prisoners in general had improved and he hoped that many 'who entered the prison with little sense of religion in their minds' had been 'induced to reflect on their past habits of immorality and crime and to forsake them in the future'. The chaplain had, however, experienced 'a greater difficulty in introducing sobriety of thought and exciting attention to religious instruction amongst the smugglers' due to 'a feverish state of mind prevalent in that class of prisoners and a persuasion that their offences are more vigorously punished than those prisoners of other classes'.

It is true smugglers were punished more harshly than many petty criminals but sentences were far less severe than for those who faced the death penalty for burglary, or transportation for stealing bread. The usual penalty for smuggling was a fine which, during the post-Napoleonic period, was about £100, with an indefinite period of imprisonment in default. Few smugglers were able to pay such an enormous sum (equivalent then to about four years' wages for an ordinary job) but most were released from prison after a year or so. There is no known record of any Dorset smuggler being hanged for a straightforward smuggling offence, though a handful were sentenced to death for offences of violence against the Coast-guard. Most of these were eventually reprieved.

There was certainly a belief among smugglers that they were being penalised for something which few people regarded as a true crime, but a contributory factor to this discontent may well have been the cramped and spartan conditions of St. Peter's Palace, as they called the county gaol. Most of the men were outdoor types – sailors, fishermen, farm labourers and so on – and prolonged confinement would have been extremely hard; not as hard, however, as it must have seemed to those arriving a few decades earlier: Dorchester was given a new prison in 1787, the old one being in a 'ruinous and insecure state', but within three years of its completion, the new building was condemned for being damp and unwholesome. Its cells were not properly ventilated, the courtyards were too small, its walls were insecure and built of ill-chosen materials, and debtors shared cells with murderers. At least women prisoners were segregated from men (which wasn't always the case) but the general conditions were considered a danger to the inmates' physical and moral health and in 1788, plans were prepared for a second replacement prison. This building, completed in 1795, was still no holiday camp but was a great improvement on previous efforts.

2 Composition   (Recommended time: 1 hour)

Plan and write a composition of about 350 words on the following:

'Widespread unemployment is largely responsible for the present increase in crime.' Discuss.

TEST   **LISTENING COMPREHENSION** (Time: approx. 20 minutes)

PART 1

For questions 1–5, complete the blanks in the statements. For questions 6–10, complete the missing information in the table.

1 One house is burgled in Britain every ....
2 In 1982 the number of houses burgled was .... more than in 1979.
3 In 1982 household burglary losses rose by ....
4 The number of burglaries *not* reported to the police is thought to be as high as .... of the total.
5 It is calculated that a house will be burgled ....

BURGLARIES IN BRITAIN: 1982		
6	Aborted attempts:	...........%
7	Loss of property £0–£5:	...........%
8	Loss of property £ ....–£ .... :	22%
9	Loss of property £ ....–£ .... :	13%
10	Loss of property over £500:	...........%

PART 2

For questions 11–22, complete the missing information in the table.

	A	B	C	D	E	F
	Receptions per 100,000	**12** .... (in years)	Overall prison population	Overall receptions	**13** .... (millions)	Prison population per 100,000
England & Wales	69	0.714	**18**...............	34002	49.00	49.55
France	**14**...............	**16**...............	13348	10272	**20**...............	25.18
Netherlands	127	**17**...............	2327	**19**...............	13.50	17.23
Scotland	**15**...............	0.359	2441	6793	5.25	46.49
Sweden	121	0.415	4152	9991	8.25	**21**...............
Switzerland	100	0.332	2157	6496	6.50	33.18
11...............	60	1.377	1235	897	1.50	**22**...............

5 Consumer Society

1 Discuss

'Only when you have bought a machine which polishes your kitchen floor in five minutes flat will you begin to wonder why you've spent years on your knees scrubbing it with soap and water! It's efficient, labour-saving and inexpensive!'

So run the advertisers' claims for gadgets, new inventions or labour-saving devices, as they are often called.

What gadgets or labour-saving devices have you or your family got at home? In groups, list as many as you can (using a dictionary if necessary), and then briefly discuss how useful they are.

2 In the Proficiency Paper 5 (Interview) you will have to answer questions about a picture and discuss related topics.

1 Study some of the ways in which we ask for a repetition, etc.

Asking for repetition	I'm sorry, I didn't quite catch } {that. understand} {what you said. Would you mind repeating it/the question/saying that again, please.
Asking for clarification	I'm sorry. I (still) don't understand what you mean. Did you want me to (describe the woman)? (= polite form of 'Do you want me to . . . ?')
Asking for time to think	(Um), let me think (a moment). If you'll just give me a moment (to gather my thoughts).

Assumption	As far as I can see, . . . / Presumably . . . I assume/presume (that) . . .
Appearance	He seems/appears to . . . / It seems/appears that . . . Apparently . . . / It/He looks as if/as though . . .
Doubt or Uncertainty	I doubt whether . . . / I don't (really) think (that) . . . I'm not really sure if/whether . . .
Certainty	It's quite clear/obvious to me (that) . . . (Quite) clearly/obviously . . . I'm quite sure/convinced (that) . . .
Expressing ignorance	I'm afraid I can't quite make out what I'm not quite sure what } . . . I'm afraid I don't know/have no idea what

2 In pairs, ask and answer the 'About the photo' and 'Personal' questions opposite, using the above as and when necessary.

NORMAN CONQUESTS:

Gadget people Richard and Barbara Norman, with daughter Victoria, are masters of all they survey. Their home contains gadgetry galore – and they are soon moving to a larger home, with even more.

1 One cup electric kettle
2 Camera with power winder
3 Pancake maker (electric)
4 Wireless remote control unit for video
5 Zoom lens for camera
6 Electric knife sharpener and can opener
7 Lawn trimmer
8 Cordless telephone
9 Facial sauna
10 Microwave oven
11 Hostess trolley
12 Turbodryer (for hair)
13 Electric toothbrush
14 Sandwich toaster
15 Musical alarm clock
16 Calculator
17 Remote control for television
18 Air freshener
19 Electric carving knife
20 Diplomat chess game
21 Pocket razor
22 Portable television

3 In small groups, discuss the questions for general discussion below.
Use these expressions as and when necessary:

Opinions	In my opinion, . . . / In my view, . . .
and	My own opinion/view/feeling is that . . .
feelings	I believe/feel/think (that) . . .
	I rather think (that) . . . / I would think (that) . . .
	I would say (that) . . . / I would have said (that) . . .

4 Now write more questions about the photo below under three headings
('About the photo', 'Personal', 'General Discussion') and in pairs ask
each other the questions.

About the photo

1 Who do you think these people are?
2 Why do you think they look so happy?
3 What are all those things on the table?
4 What's that thing (number 1)? What do you think it's for?
5 Why do you think the photo was taken?

Personal

1 Would you like to have as many gadgets as the Normans?

2 Have you or your family got any of these?
3 Is this your idea of happiness?

General discussion

1 Are gadgets necessary? Do they save or make work? What about the energy they use?
2 What kinds of people *really* benefit from gadgets and labour-saving devices?
3 It's said we live in 'a throwaway society'. What do you think?

Grammar

1 Compound nouns and relative pronouns *which, who* and *that*

Whenever we mention or discuss inventions, gadgets, labour-saving devices and people's jobs, we often use compound nouns. And when explaining what a gadget does or what a job involves, we will often use relative pronouns.

1 Study this table and describe what each article is or what each person does, e.g.

A carving knife is a knife (which is) used for carving meat.
A knife sharpener is something/a gadget/a device which/that sharpens knives.
A bus driver is someone/a person that/who drives a bus.

a) A carving knife A frying pan A sewing machine		
b) A cooking apple Chewing gum A hearing aid		which ....
c) A coffee grinder A tin/can opener A fire extinguisher	is	
d) A wristwatch A pocket knife		that ....
e) A cordless telephone An electric toothbrush		
f) A gadget man An air hostess A language teacher A sheep farmer A bank manager A taxman A traffic warden	is	who .... that ....

What do you notice about the compound nouns in each group (a–e)? How have they been formed? Can you think of any others that are formed in the same way?

'A blasted power-cut, just as I was cleaning my teeth!'

2 **Game:** *20 Questions* (see Teacher's Guide Unit 5)

2 Participle *-ing* form as subject to replace a *Since/As/Because/When* . . . clause

Study this, then do the exercise:

Being a busy housewife, you can't do without a vacuum cleaner.	= Since/As/Because you are a busy housewife, you can't do without a vacuum cleaner.
Not having much time for housework, you could do with a washing machine.	= Since you don't have much time for housework, you could do with a washing machine.
Having used our coffee grinder once, you'll never use anything else.	= When you have used our coffee grinder once, you'll never use anything else!
Not/Never having had a machine like this before, you'll be absolutely amazed at what it can do!	= Since you have not/never had a machine like this before, you'll be absolutely amazed at what it can do!

NOTE: When this participle construction is used, the subject of both halves of the sentence MUST be the same.

Rephrase each of the following sentences using a participle construction:

1 As I don't know the 'best buy' myself, I'll take your advice.
2 Since I've just bought a new wristwatch, I ought to get to my appointments on time now.
3 As he's not a very technical person, he couldn't understand it.
4 Since she's never had a dishwasher, she won't miss it.
5 Because I agreed to help with the party, I thought I'd better get there early.

3 Present participle *-ing* form for clause or sentence substitution.

Study this, then do the exercise below:

1a While I was waiting to be served, I looked at the record players.
1b ⟶ While waiting to be served, I looked at the record players.
2a When I plugged the machine in, I got an electric shock.
2b → On plugging the machine in, I got an electric shock.
3a He stayed at home and cleaned the flat.
3b → He stayed at home, cleaning the flat.

In 1b, what other word could be used in place of *while*?
In 2b, what other word could be used instead of *on*?
Why is *on* used in 2b but not in 3b? What is the difference in the reference to time?

NOTE: Again, this construction can only be used when the subject of both clause and sentence is the same.

Convert these sentences to this present participle construction, using the words given:

1 While we do everything we can to dispatch orders quickly, we can't work miracles! (*While . . .*)
2 It moves smoothly across any lawn and picks up all the leaves. (–)
3 When you hear the warning sound, you must immediately switch off the machine. (*On . . .*)
4 While the manufacturers recommend 'Brand X', they cannot of course insist on your using it. (*While . . .*)
5 Though I agree that *this* tin opener is quite good, I must say that *that* one is much easier to use. (*Though . . . /While . . .*)

Listening

1 You're going to hear an advertisement. Listen, then in pairs ask each other these questions:

1 What is this advertisement for?
2 What kind of people is the advertisement aimed at?
3 How does Mr James feel about it?
4 What will the machine do?
5 How much could it cost? And what else is included?
6 How long does the offer last?

2 In pairs, discuss and write a similar advertisement for another new gadget or labour-saving device e.g. a toasted sandwich maker, a coffee percolator, a sewing machine, etc. Use the kind of language you heard in the advertisement above and constructions you have practised in this and other Units.

Oral Interview preparation

1 Reading aloud

There are certain points to watch when reading aloud. We will concentrate on two here:

1 punctuation in the passage to be read; and
2 primary word stress, particularly in compound nouns.

1 As far as reading aloud is concerned, the punctuation will
   a) give you an idea of the intonation and expression needed for a complete sentence, as with, for example, a full stop (.), a question mark (?) or an exclamation mark (!); and it will also
   b) tell you when to pause: a clear pause after a full stop (.), a shorter pause after a comma (,), a colon (:), a semi-colon (;) or a dash (–).

Study these sentences, noting where to pause and deciding whether it is a plain statement, a statement with emotion or a question. Then listen and repeat.

1 This coffee percolator, which is now ten years old, is absolutely useless!
2 Have you found someone to do the job – the job I mentioned to you?
3 Having been there once, you'll never go there again!
4 Mr Jones, who's a friend of mine by the way, has just invented a new carpet sweeper.
5 We were all looking forward to the party; little did we know what we would find!

2 In this Unit we have met a number of compound nouns. Look at these and notice the way they are pronounced. The primary stress is on the first part:

a 'knife sharpener; a 'washing machine; 'chewing gum;
a 'coffee percolator; a 'carving knife; a 'wristwatch; a 'hairdryer;
a 'sheep farmer; a 'taxman

3 Now study this passage and be prepared to read it aloud.

In Victorian times the 'gadget man' would have bought those gadgets which now find their way into the Victoria and Albert Museum: the pop-up umbrella; the cigar-cum-ashtray; the penny-farthing bicycle; the roller skate; the cat's whisker wireless; the moustache press. Until 10 years ago, gadgets remained mechanical, restricted to fads like lengths of chain dangling from cars to prevent car sickness, and ashtrays which whirled dog-ends out of sight at the touch of a button.

They were mostly advertised in down-market Sunday papers: 'Do you need a haircut? Why not try the new, handy, portable Eazi-trim? Just comb your hair and – hey presto – a perfect trim! No unsightly leads or cords. No hidden extras. No batteries.' And no hair, unless you were very careful!

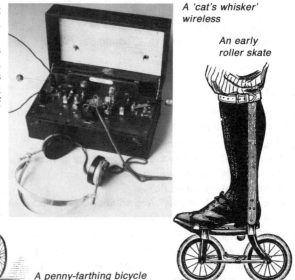

A 'cat's whisker' wireless

An early roller skate

A penny-farthing bicycle

2 Talking about a picture and discussing related topics

Study this picture* and then ask and answer the questions below in pairs.
Remember the language you used earlier in the Unit to ask for a
repetition or clarification, to express assumptions, certainty, doubt, etc.

About the photo

1 What equipment has Dick got in his study?
2 What do the various things help him do?
3 What kind of chair is he sitting in? Why?
4 Can you suggest other 'gadgets' or devices which
would make life easier for him?
5 How old do you think Dick is? What do you think he
did before he was given all this equipment?

Personal

1 How do you think you would feel if you couldn't
communicate?
2 What gadgets or machines would you like to make
your work easier?

For general discussion

1 Technology and the disabled.
2 The responsibility of the State towards the
handicapped.
3 The home of the future.

3 Game: *Just a Minute* (see Teacher's Guide Unit 5)

Homework exercise   (Recommended time: 1 hour)

Composition

'The only people who benefit from new gadgets and labour-saving
devices nowadays are the rich – and they don't need them!' Plan and
write a balanced discussion on this theme either in the form of a dialogue
between two speakers, or in essay form. (You should aim to write about
350 words.)

---

* This is a photo of Dick Boydell from Milton Keynes, England. He suffers from
cerebral palsy and had never been able to communicate until he was provided with
highly sophisticated modern technology which proved his high intelligence.

6 Science and Science Fiction

1 Which do you prefer reading, factual scientific reports or science fiction? Why? Which are your favourite science fiction writers or stories? Tell each other.

2 Did you see or read *2001: A Space Odyssey*? What did you think of it? Do you know its sequel *2010: Odyssey Two*? Read this extract from it to see if you enjoy it.

'Who is it?' whispered someone, to a chorus of shushes. Floyd raised his hands in a gesture of ignorance – and, he hoped, innocence.

'. . . know you are aboard *Leonov* . . . may not have
5 much time . . . aiming my suit antenna where I think . . .'

The signal vanished for agonizing seconds, then came back much clearer, though not appreciably louder.

'. . . relay this information to Earth. *Tsien* destroyed three hours ago. I'm only survivor. Using my suit radio – no idea if
10 it has enough range, but it's the only chance. Please listen carefully. THERE IS LIFE ON EUROPA I repeat: THERE IS LIFE ON EUROPA . . .'

The signal faded again. A stunned silence followed that no one attempted to interrupt. While he was waiting, Floyd
15 searched his memory furiously. He could not recognize the voice – it might have been that of any Western-educated Chinese. Probably it was someone he had met at a scientific conference, but unless the speaker identified himself he would never know.
20 '. . . soon after local midnight. We were pumping steadily and the tanks were almost half full. Dr Lee and I went out to check the pipe insulation. *Tsien* stands – stood – about thirty metres from the edge of the Grand Canal. Pipes go directly from it and down through the ice. Very thin – not
25 safe to walk on. The warm upwelling . . .'

Again a long silence. Floyd wondered if the speaker was moving, and had been momentarily cut off by some obstruction.

'. . . no problem – five kilowatts of lighting strung up on
30 the ship. Like a Christmas tree – beautiful, shining right through the ice. Glorious colours. Lee saw it first – a huge dark mass rising up from the depths. At first we thought it was a school of fish – too large for a single organism – then it started to break through the ice.
35 'Dr Floyd, I hope you can hear me. This is Professor Chang – we met in '02 – Boston IAU conference.'

Instantly, incongruously, Floyd's thoughts were a billion kilometres away. He vaguely remembered that reception, after the closing session of the International Astronomical
40 Union Congress – the last one that the Chinese had attended before the Second Cultural Revolution. And now he recalled Chang very distinctly – a small humorous

astronomer and exobiologist with a good fund of jokes. He wasn't joking now.
45 '. . . like huge strands of wet seaweed, crawling along the ground. Lee ran back to the ship to get a camera – I stayed to watch, reporting over the radio. The thing moved so slowly I could easily outrun it. I was much more excited than alarmed. Thought I knew what kind of creature it was – I've
50 seen pictures of the kelp forests off California – but I was quite wrong.

'. . . I could tell it was in trouble. It couldn't possibly survive at a temperature a hundred and fifty below its normal environment. It was freezing solid as it moved
55 forward – bits were breaking off like glass – but it was still advancing toward the ship, a black tidal wave, slowing down all the time.

'I was still so surprised that I couldn't think straight and I couldn't imagine what it was trying to do . . .'

Did you enjoy the extract? Why?/Why not? Do you now want to read the book?

3 Skimming

Where are all the characters who are mentioned in the extract? What are they all doing?

4 Reading for detail

Read these multiple-choice questions and choose which you think is the correct answer in each – A, B, C or D. Work out why you think the other choices are wrong. Then in small groups discuss and justify your answers.

1 Who said: 'Who is it?'?

  A Floyd.
  B Leonov.
  C Professor Chang.
  D One of the crew. ✓

2 What is *Tsien*?
  A A planet.
  B A town.
  C A space ship. ✓
  D A monstrous creature.

3 The life form on Europa is

  A a type of fish.
  B a kind of seaweed.
  C an unknown species. ✓
  D a kind of mobile tree.

4 The creature kept moving towards the ship because

  A it was carried in on a wave.
  B it knew the men were terrified.
  C it was attracted by the lights. ✓
  D it had to use the tunnel of ice.

5 How did Lee and Chang feel when they saw the creature?
  A They felt very interested. ✓
  B They felt sorry for the creature.
  C They were too scared to do anything.
  D They wanted to take photographs of the creature.

5 Guessing the meaning of words from context

Find the following words in the extract and, in pairs, work out their meaning from the context:

range; faded; stunned; tanks; crawling; kelp; buckle; topple

6 Discussion

1 How do you think this episode might end? Why?
2 Why do you think science fiction has become so popular?
3 Can science fiction help science in any way?

60   'Is there any way we can call him back?' Floyd whispered urgently.

    'No – it's too late, Europa will soon be behind Jupiter. We'll have to wait until it comes out of eclipse.'

    '. . . climbing up the ship, building a kind of ice tunnel as it
65 advanced. Perhaps this was insulating it from the cold – the way termites protect themselves from the sunlight with their little corridors of mud.

    '. . . tons of ice on the ship. The radio antennas broke off first. Then I could see the landing legs beginning to buckle –
70 all in slow motion, like a dream.

    'Not until the ship started to topple did I realize what the thing was trying to do – and then it was too late. We could have saved ourselves – if we'd only switched off those lights.'

Vocabulary in reading

1 Differences in meaning

In Section A of the Proficiency Paper 1 (Reading Comprehension) there are multiple-choice questions which ask you to distinguish between words in the same vocabulary area, e.g.

The meeting was .... to a later date.
A postponed   B cancelled   C delayed   D held up

These are clearly all verbs connected with changing arrangements, but 'postponed' must be correct because a meeting *can't* be 'cancelled', 'delayed' or 'held up' *to a later date.*

Here are some other vocabulary areas related to three verbs taken from the extract on pages 36–37.

Group work

Study these tables and, using a dictionary where necessary, work out how the verbs differ in meaning by making true sentences. *Do not add any other words.*

1   *to topple:* some related verbs – *to slump, to tumble, to capsize, to sink*

These verbs are all connected with the concept of 'falling'.

fall down quite violently

A boat		sink.
A building	can	tumble.
A person		topple.
Sales figures	cannot	capsize.
		slump.

T U M B L E

2   *to fade:* some related verbs – *to dim, to glimmer, to die away, to flicker*

These verbs are all connected with the concept of 'losing strength, colour, etc.'.

A signal		fade.
A light	can	dim.
A candle		glimmer.
A voice	cannot	die away.
A colour		flicker.

FADE

diamond glitter
light glimmer (v. weakly)

3   *to crawl:* some related verbs – *to creep, to trickle, to ooze, to stroll*

These verbs are all connected with the concept of 'moving slowly'.

Water		crawl.
Mud	can	creep.
A baby		trickle.
A person	cannot	ooze.
An insect		stroll.

ooze – cieknąć
trickle – dripping
gushing – a great quantity of water

walking along

2 Vocabulary areas

1 Meet Arthur C. Clarke, the author of *2001: A Space Odyssey* and *2010: Odyssey Two* and find three examples in the text which seem to justify the article's headline.

Arthur C. Clarke: fiction spilling over into fact

When the Apollo 8 astronauts became the first men ever to see the far side of the Moon, they were reportedly tempted to radio back to earth the discovery of a large black monolith on the lunar surface.

'Alas discretion prevailed', Arthur C. Clarke says now with only the faintest hint of a smile. If they had, few people would have been completely surprised, for it was Clarke's brilliant fictional creation of space travel in his novel *2001: A Space Odyssey* which not only provided a generation with its image of space exploration, but also predicted the existence of inexplicable monoliths on other planets.

It was an imaginative vision which made Clarke the most successful science fiction writer of all time, and among the richest writers in the world.

Today the sequel to his original breath-taking vision of the future of man in space, called *2010: Odyssey Two*, is published in England. There seems little doubt it will provide a new generation with its imaginative space vocabulary.

But although Clarke's work is fiction, it seems forever on the very edge of fact. 'Sometimes I think my prophecies are almost self-fulfilling,' he says. 'Do you know they have even found something in the rings of Saturn that they can't explain. It's a very small intense source of radio noise and one theory is that it's an artefact.'

He can hardly conceal his glee that he predicted it in his first novel.

When *2001* was first written at the urging of the film director Stanley Kubrick, who wanted to use it as the basis of 'the proverbial good science fiction movie' and went on to do so with spectacular success, the moons of Io, Europa, Ganymede and Callisto were mere pinpoints of light to even the most powerful telescope. This did not prevent Clarke describing them, and now since the Voyager space probes they are defined worlds. 'They are even beginning to discuss the theory that there is life on Europa', Clarke says as again he had hinted in *2001*.

In the 14 years since *2001* was published, Clarke has always maintained it was impossible to write a sequel. Indeed five years ago he even announced that he was retiring as a writer after more than 60 of his books had been published and sold 20 million copies throughout the world.

'But something in my subconcious told me that I couldn't. I wanted to see what was on the other side of the next hill, to find out what happened'.

So he sat down and wrote a 10-page synopsis of what happened to the crew of the spaceship Discovery in *2001*.

'I sent it to my agent and he phoned me back at once to tell me I couldn't leave it like that. If I'd write a sequel he'd get me a million dollars for it in 24 hours'. Clarke decided to go back to the word processor which has now replaced his typewriter.

(November 4, 1982)

2 Building vocabulary areas: Write on a piece of paper these three headings for three columns:

SPACE VOCABULARY	WRITING/AUTHORSHIP VOCABULARY	ADJECTIVES OF PRAISE

Then read through the article again carefully and complete your columns with relevant vocabulary from it.

3 What other words do you yourselves know that you could add to the columns? In pairs, add as many as you can and then compare your lists with the rest of the class.

3 Collocation

1   Read this passage about *Pioneer 10*, noting down *Pioneer*'s achievements.

Pioneer 10 pushes beyond goals, into the unknown

By John Noble Wilford

New York — Out there, far, far away where Earth is a mere pinpoint of light and the Sun is a pale disk of diminishing consequence, a hardy little spacecraft cruises on and on into the unexplored. No machine of human design has ever gone so far. Pioneer 10 has traveled to the reaches of Pluto, a distance it achieved April 25, and is advancing toward the edge of the solar system.

From out there, now 2.7 billion miles away, Pioneer's eight-watt radio transmitter sends faint messages back to Earth every day.

Scientists with the patience to extract the signals out of the background noise and to decipher their messages are learning for the first time what it is like in the outermost solar system. It is cold and dark and empty, as they knew it must be. A tenuous wind of solar particles, the million-mile-an-hour solar wind, still blows outward. Cosmic rays race inward.

If the spacecraft survives long enough and the scientists are clever enough, more exciting discoveries could lie ahead for Pioneer 10. The spacecraft might be able to detect gravity waves, which have been theorized but have never been observed. It might locate the source of the mysterious force tugging at Uranus and Neptune, a force suggesting the presence of some as yet unseen object.

When Pioneer 10 was launched March 3, 1972, from Cape Canaveral, Florida, no spacecraft had ventured farther than Mars. Pioneer flew within 81,000 miles of Jupiter's cloudtops on Dec. 2, 1973, returning the first close-up images of the Sun's largest planet. Pioneer made the first detailed observations of Jupiter's powerful radiation belts and discovered that the planet's sphere of magnetic influence extended to the orbit of Saturn, a distance of half a billion miles.

Pioneer had by then accomplished its mission and exceeded its designed 21-month lifetime. Still it kept going, its nine-foot dish antenna always cocked in the direction of Earth.

It is estimated that deep-space antennas should maintain communications with Pioneer for another eight years, out to a distance of 5 billion miles.

Pioneer is now, in effect, leaving the realm of the known planets. On June 13, Pioneer's outbound trajectory will cross Neptune's orbit, 2.81 billion miles from the Sun. Normally Pluto is the outermost planet, but its orbit is highly elliptical, unlike the roughly circular orbits of the other planets, so Pluto is now nearer the Sun than Neptune and will be for the next 17 years.

2   Read the passage again and extract more 'space vocabulary' to add to your lists.

3   Collocation is very common in language and gives it much of its 'natural feel'. Many of the vocabulary answers in Section A of the Proficiency Paper 1 (Reading Comprehension) depend on correct collocation.

According to the *Longman Dictionary of Contemporary English*, the verb *to collocate* = 'to go together or with another word in a way which sounds natural': 'strong' collocates with 'coffee' but 'powerful' does not. The words 'strong' and 'coffee' collocate.

Here are some examples of collocation taken from the passage above:

a *pinpoint* of light	— NOT a drop, a fleck or a dot
the Sun is a *pale* disk	— NOT faint, dim or colourless
a *faint* message	— NOT slight, soft or low
accomplished its mission	— NOT succeeded or fulfilled

From the point of view of meaning, the words on the right would make sense, but they *do not collocate* with the other words, so they don't sound natural in English.

4   Find in the relevant passages the correct collocations for the following:
   a) *2010: Odyssey Two* (pp.36–37): the signal _____ (*2 possible*); a _____ silence; a _____ of fish; a _____ of jokes; I couldn't think _____
   b) *Arthur C. Clarke* (p.39): the _____ side of the Moon; the _____ of a smile; to _____ his glee; a mere _____ of light

   NOTE: There are no magic rules for learning word collocations. Each collocation has to be learned separately, so watch out for them in everything you read from now on!

5   Discussion
   Is space exploration worth the vast fortunes that are spent on it?

May 5, 1983

Grammar

Present Perfect, Simple Past and Past Perfect Tenses

1 Look at these examples of tense use taken from the text on Pioneer 10:

1 *Present Perfect*
No machine of human design *has ever gone* so far.
Pioneer 10 *has travelled* to the reaches of Pluto.
. . . gravity waves which *have been theorized* but
have never been observed.

2 *Simple Past*
It is cold and dark and empty, as they *knew* it must
be.
When Pioneer 10 *was launched* March 3, 1972, . . .
Pioneer *made* the first detailed observations of
Jupiter's radiation belts . . .

3 *Past Perfect*
When Pioneer 10 was launched . . . , no
spacecraft *had ventured* farther than Mars.
Pioneer *had by then accomplished* its mission and
(had) exceeded . . .

2 Now decide whether the following statements are true or false:

1 The Simple Past is only used with actions whose date is given. *F*
2 The Simple Past is used for all actions that occurred before now. *F*
3 The Simple Past is used for completed actions or states. *T*
4 The Past Perfect is used to show that one past action happened before something else in the past. *T*
5 The Past Perfect must be accompanied by the Simple Past. *F*

6 The Past Perfect is used to talk about states (or actions) that occurred a very long time ago. *F*
7 The Present Perfect is used for completed past actions which are recent and have no time mentioned. *T*
8 The Present Perfect refers to long actions. *F*
9 The Present Perfect has no relationship with present time. *F*
10 The Present Perfect relates past actions to the present. *T*

3 Put the verbs in the following sentences in the correct tense:

1 The fact that Pioneer has survived so long *has delighted* (to delight) scientists.
2 Before Pioneer, no spacecraft *had travelled* (to travel) so far.
3 No human being *has visited* (to visit) Jupiter yet.
4 I can't remember when the first men *set foot* (to set foot) on the Moon.
5 I *have seen* (to see) so many satellites I don't even look for them now.

6 It *was launched* (to launch) a couple of years ago.
7 That moment *was* (to be) one of the most exciting I've known.
8 Although she *has stopped* (to stop) writing science fiction stories her books are still very popular.
9 No sooner *had it gone* (it/to go) into orbit than its signal faded.
10 Up till then, scientists *had* (to have) no proof of their theories.

4 General Knowledge Quiz: True or False?

How good is your general knowledge?
Put a 'T' for true or an 'F' for false against the numbers 1–5 on a piece of paper.

1 The Russians have never set foot on the Moon.
2 Yuri Gagarin flew in the first Sputnik in 1966.
3 India has had a space programme for ten years.

4 Before Jules Verne no one had ever foreseen space flights.
5 Before 1973 no one had ever stepped on the Moon.

Now discuss your answers with the rest of the class. Who knew most?

Write other sentences similar to those above about space exploration so far, then test the knowledge of other members of the class. Your sentences can be true or false, but you at least must be sure of the right answer!

TEST   **READING COMPREHENSION**   (Time: 30 minutes)

SECTION A

In this section you must choose the word or phrase which best completes each sentence. For each question, 1 to 15, indicate on a piece of paper the letter A, B, C or D against the number of the question.

1 For years she had .... of meeting her long-lost sister.

   A hoped   B wished   C longed   D dreamed

2 When I applied for my passport, I had to send my birth .... with the application.

   A proof   B certificate   C paper   D document

3 The .... against your having that kind of accident are about 500 to 1.

   A possibilities   B figures   C opportunities   D odds

4 They live in a .... house in the suburbs of London.

   A single   B detached   C free-standing   D distinct

5 The children were .... with a family far from their parents' home.

   A reared   B brought up   C bred   D grown up

6 Many people these days find it difficult to .... a career.

   A settle into   B stabilise   C settle down   D arrange

7 They shared out the .... of the business among all the partners.

   A makings   B proceedings   C benefits   D proceeds

8 .... all his problems he never allowed himself to get depressed.

   A As for   B Despite   C Nevertheless   D Granted

9 No one was capable of breaking the .... silence following the news.

   A harsh   B thick   C stunned   D punched

10 They noticed a flame .... in the breeze.

   A flickering   B flashing   C blinking   D sparkling

11 .... being a scientist, he also wrote fiction.

   A Owing to   B According to   C Whereas   D Besides

12 He congratulated his opponent with just a .... of a smile on his face.

   A mark   B print   C hint   D sign

13 The signal was extremely difficult to ....

   A settle   B decipher   C capture   D fix

14 He never expected his prophecy to be ....

   A accomplished   B realised   C achieved   D fulfilled

15 They haven't discovered any new planets ....

   A recently   B previously   C last year   D shortly

42

SECTION B

In this section you will find after the passage a number of questions or unfinished statements about it, each with four suggested answers or ways of finishing. You must choose the one which you think fits best. For each question, 16 to 20, indicate on your piece of paper the letter A, B, C or D against the number of the question.

SOMEWHERE above, hidden by the eternal clouds of Wesker's World, a thunder rumbled and grew. Trader John Garth stopped when he heard it, his boots sinking slowly into the muck, and cupped his good ear to catch the sound. It swelled and waned in the thick atmosphere, growing louder.

'That noise is the same as the noise of your sky-ship,' Itin said, with stolid Wesker logicality, slowly pulverizing the idea in his mind and turning over the bits one by one for closer examination. 'But your ship is still sitting where you landed it. It must be, even though we cannot see it, because you are the only one who can operate it. And even if anyone else could operate it we would have heard it rising into the sky. Since we did not, and if this sound is a sky-ship sound, then it must mean . . .'

'Yes, another ship,' Garth said, too absorbed in his own thoughts to wait for the laborious Weskerian chains of logic to clank their way through to the end. Of course it was another spacer, it had been only a matter of time before one appeared, and undoubtedly this one was homing on the S.S. radar reflector as he had done. His own ship would show up clearly on the newcomer's screen and they would probably set down as close to it as they could.

'You better go ahead, Itin,' he said. 'Use the water so you can get to the village quickly. Tell everyone to get back into the swamps, well clear of the hard ground. That ship is landing on instruments and anyone underneath at touchdown is going to be cooked.'

This immediate threat was clear enough to the little Wesker amphibian. Before Garth finished speaking Itin's ribbed ears had folded like a bat's wing and he slipped silently into the nearby canal. Garth squelched on through the mud, making as good time as he could over the clinging surface. He had just reached the fringes of the village clearing when the rumbling grew to a head-splitting roar and the spacer broke through the low-hanging layer of clouds above. Garth shielded his eyes from the down-reaching tongue of flame and examined the growing form of the grey-black ship with mixed feelings.

16 Why did John Garth 'cup his good ear'?

A Because it was thundering.
B He thought there was a storm coming.
C To listen more closely to the noise.
D Because he could hardly hear what Itin was saying.

17 What does the text tell us about Itin and Garth?

A They reasoned in the same way.
B They came to the same conclusion.
C They were rude to each other.
D They helped each other's thoughts along.

18 After they heard the noise, Itin

A swam back to the village.
B walked to the swamps.
C flew back over the swamp to the village.
D ran back to the village over the hard ground.

19 What do we know definitely about Itin?

A He came from the same village as Garth.
B He wore a special amphibious suit.
C His surname was Wesker.
D He was an inhabitant of the planet Wesker.

20 Garth knew another spacer had come because

A he was half expecting one.
B he saw it on his screen.
C he was more intelligent than Itin.
D he recognised its landing instruments.

7 The Energy Debate

1 Look at this picture and answer the questions.

What does this picture make you think about?

What are the advantages and disadvantages of farming by this method?

Would it be worth farming like this to save energy?

2 Read the two letters below and answer these questions:

Do they say the same thing? How are they different? Why do the two letters employ such different styles? What do these styles tell us about each writer's attitude towards his reader?

Dear Sir,
   I read your article in Tuesday's "Times" with considerable amazement. I'm afraid that if, as your article would seem to suggest, you are seriously proposing that the bullock and human muscle power be re-introduced as farming methods, the proposal cannot be given any serious consideration.
   There can be no doubt that bullocks do in fact permit savings in fuel and fertiliser, as well as being non-pollutant, cheap and contributing to soil quality. However, it would surely not be called progress to force men to return to back-breaking labour, nor would anyone these days be prepared to undertake this kind of work.
   I also have strong reservations as to the bullock's productivity in comparison with that of a tractor.
   No, Sir, I fear that your proposal can only lead to hard work, poor productivity and more imports, a situation I fail to see any advantage in.

   I remain,
   Yours faithfully,

Dear Sir,
   When I read your article the other day I was horrified.
   Are you seriously suggesting we should start farming with bullocks and human muscle power again? With all respect, you must be out of your tiny mind!
   Yes, I'm sure we'd save on fuel and fertilisers, and sure that bullocks are cheap and good for the soil and don't pollute, either, but do you really think you can make people do back-breaking work again and call that progress? And, anyway, who do you think you'd find these days willing to do work like that? Not me, for one!
   I'd like to know, too, just how productive a bullock is. How many fields can it plough in a day? Not half as many as a tractor, I bet!
   Apparently you'd be quite happy to send us back to the fields, ... but to produce less so we'd have to import more? What's the sense in that?

   Yours faithfully,

44

I know him when I lived ~~to~~ thX
y've known him nix years

3 The two letters at the bottom of page 44 are examples of 'formal' and 'informal' written English. In pairs or small groups, work out how the language of the two styles differs.

4 Now study this table and find examples in the letters of the features mentioned.

FORMAL WRITTEN ENGLISH tends to use . . .	INFORMAL WRITTEN ENGLISH tends to use . . .

1 Longer sentences linked by joining words.
2 More varied joining words.
3 A less personal style:
  – use of Passive constructions.
  – use of Conditional sentences.
  – use of introductory phrases.
  – use of explicit reasoning.
4 More exact vocabulary.
5 Latin origin vocabulary
  e.g. *occupation.*
6 Nouns or adjectives to replace verbs
  e.g. *possible, possibility.*
7 More non-contracted verb forms.
	1 Shorter sentences and shorter paragraphs.
	2 Simple joining words (*and, but,* etc.).
	3 A more direct, personal style:
	  – use of Active constructions.
	  – use of Present tenses.
	  – little use of introductory phrases.
	  – use of rhetorical questions.
	4 Vaguer vocabulary.
	5 Anglo-Saxon vocabulary
	  e.g. *job.*
	6 Greater use of verbs
	  e.g. *may, might.*
	7 More contracted verb forms e.g. *can't.*

5 Imagine that you have been asked to write letters in reply to those on page 44. Your letters will contain points 1–6 below. Before writing the letters, note down the language appropriate for each point in the letter according to the style and register necessary (formal or informal).

	FORMAL	INFORMAL
1 Thank writer for letter.		
2 Apologise for not writing before.		
3 State disagreement with ideas expressed in writer's letter.		
4 Give reasons for disagreement.		
5 Invite writer to see your farm.		
6 Close letter.		

6 Write the two letters for homework, concentrating on the style and register of each. (Recommended time for homework: 30 minutes)

7 Discussion

Are there any fields in which we could save energy by making greater use of *human* energy? If so, what are they? And would it be worth it? What do you think?

Directed writing

The Directed Writing Composition exercise in the Proficiency Paper 2 (Composition) often requires you to expand some given information into, for example, a letter, a report, an article or a conversation. It may also require you to use an appropriate style of language i.e. formal or informal, and to express some degree of approval or disapproval.

Below are some examples of this kind of composition. Read each carefully, then discuss and decide exactly what kind of expansion work, what style and what tone each requires.

1

SEPTEMBER MUSIC FESTIVAL

– SOMETHING FOR EVERBODY'S TASTES
– ANY TIME OF THE DAY OR NIGHT
– CATERING AND CAMPING FACILITIES PROVIDED

COME ALONG!   YOU'LL LOVE IT!

As the music critic for your newspaper you went to the second day of this 30-day festival to judge it. You were highly impressed by everything you saw. Write an article praising all the different aspects of the festival and fully recommending it to readers.

2 You are an English teacher looking for a job. You see the following ad in a newspaper and are appalled by what you judge to be its sex and age prejudice. Write a letter to the Director of the school protesting, giving your reasons and threatening legal action in certain circumstances.

SITUATION VACANT

Teacher of English, private language school. Must speak English fluently and have at least 3 years' relevant experience. Preference will be given to female candidates between ages 22 and 25. For further details, write . . .

3 You are a journalist and come into work one Monday morning to find that your editor has left this note on your desk:

Govt. cuts close down only Secondary School in area - children will be obliged to travel 20 miles to nearest school - poor transport - nearest school has poor reputation - local authorities and local population up in arms over situation. Please enquire.

You immediately jump into your car and drive off to the town concerned to get more information so as to be able to write an article on the situation for your paper. You arrive at the town to find a public meeting in progress protesting against the Government's decision. After the meeting you manage to interview Mrs Joan Hepworth, a mother and the fiery, outspoken and angry leader of the protest movement.

Write the interview that takes place between you and Mrs Hepworth.

4

```
Mr A. Jackson,                              19 Scotts Hill,
The Secretary,                              Shalpool.
Hartley Old Age Pensioners' Club,
Hartley,                                    1st March 198-
Bloomwich.


Dear Mr Jackson,
       Many thanks for inviting me to talk at your club on the subject
'Censorship is essential in today's TV and cinema', an issue which,
as you know, I wholeheartedly support.  I enclose an outline
(approximately 300 words) of my intended speech.  I would be most
grateful if you could read through it to judge its suitability for
your audience who I understand will be mainly widowed ladies.
       I look forward to hearing from you.
                          Yours sincerely,
```

Write the outline of the intended speech to which you referred in the above letter.

The language of approval and disapproval

1 Read the expressions below and decide whether they are formal or
informal. Put an 'F' (for formal) or an 'I' (for informal) in the brackets
against each one or on a piece of paper. Some of the expressions may
be both.

1 I would like to say how absolutely disgusted I was . . . ( )
2 It was great! ( )
3 Thanks a lot. ( )
4 I would like to express my extreme disapproval . . . ( )
5 My sincere congratulations on . . . ( )
6 It was most satisfactory. ( )
7 I must register a strong complaint. ( )
8 I wish to report how extremely satisfied I was . . . ( )
9 What excellent service! ( )
10 I was utterly horrified . . . ( )
11 First class! ( )
12 You've no idea how upset I was . . . ( )
13 How delighted I am that . . . ( )
14 I really must complain . . . ( )
15 I regret that I have no choice but to write to . . . ( )
16 Congratulations on . . . ( )
17 I really was pleased . . . ( )
18 I found it amazingly good. ( )

2 Now work in pairs and write out the above expressions under two
columns:

EXPRESSIONS OF APPROVAL	EXPRESSIONS OF DISAPPROVAL

3 Vocabulary building

Complete the lists below by adding to them any other adjectives you
know to express the same kinds of ideas:

disgusted, horrified, upset, ...
delighted, pleased, satisfied, ...

Then compare your list with another student, adding to either as appropriate.

4 Collocation

Referring to Unit 4 (p.27), decide which adverbs you can use with the above
adjectives to reinforce them, e.g. *utterly disgusted*, *absolutely delighted*, etc.

Listening

1 You are going to hear a formal discussion about nuclear energy.

1 Listen to it once and then answer this question:
   What are the positions held by the two speakers?

2 Now listen to it again and note, in two columns on a piece of paper,
   the arguments employed FOR and AGAINST nuclear energy.

3 Now, in pairs or small groups, compare and complete your notes.
   (NOTE: Don't lose them. You'll need them in exercise **3**.)

2 Vocabulary

In two groups, listen to the discussion again. This time, each group
listens for a different reason:

Group 1: Students note down all the expressions the speakers use as
          general rejections of the other speaker's arguments.

Group 2: Students note down the words or phrases in the discussion
          which mean the same as the following:

1 to operate (a nuclear power plant)   6 confused
2 to fail to see or to disregard   7 (to consider) a point
3 very high (expenditure)   8 the greatest (care)
4 to consider   9 to mark or disfigure
5 in my opinion   10 to risk (catching)

Now in pairs (each pair consisting of one student from each group above), exchange your findings.

3 Reconstructing the discussion / Role play

In pairs, and using the FOR and AGAINST notes you made in **1** (2 and 3) above, reconstruct the discussion
orally.

4 Discussion

What do *you* really think? Which speaker do you agree with most? Why?
What viable solutions are there to the energy shortage?

*Sellafield
nuclear
power station*

Style

Below is an imaginary newspaper headline and two imaginary letters written to the newspaper commenting on the article which followed the headline.

1 Before filling in the blanks, read both letters and discuss what position they adopt, their tone and what style they are written in.

2 Complete the blanks in each letter. Only one word is missing in each blank.

GOVT. GIVES GO-AHEAD TO NUCLEAR PLANT

Dear Sir,
  It was with the *utmost* __(1)__ dismay that I read yesterday of the Government decision to go *ahead* __(2)__ with the construction of a nuclear power *station* __(3)__. I can *only* __(4)__ see this decision as a great step backwards for mankind. Nowhere in the world *have* __(5)__ anyone been able to guarantee the safety of nuclear plants *and* __(6)__ find an adequate method of disposing of nuclear waste. *Yet* __(7)__ the Government seems to be willing to *expose* __(8)__ its population to such risks.
  I *have* __(9)__ to say on behalf of my children and myself that we cannot accept this decision and we have no choice *but* __(10)__ to register a strong protest against this decision. We __(11)__ hope that others will join us in this protest so that sufficient pressure is put on the Government to make *them* __(12)__ think again and wisely change their minds.

Dear Sir,
  Congratulations! Congratulations to your newspaper for your hard-fought campaign and *also* __(1)__ to the Government *for* __(2)__ its decision to adopt nuclear power. This is one of the most sensible decisions this Government has *made* __(3)__. Now at *last* __(4)__ we can look forward *to* __(5)__ a guaranteed supply of cheap energy with no worries about what happens the day coal and gas run out. *How* __(6)__ delighted I am that people's unfounded and emotional fears have been overcome, *that* __(7)__ our industry can look forward to a secure energy supply and *so* __(8)__ that the man *in* __(9)__ the street won't have to put up __(10)__ *with* any restrictions on his personal consumption.

electricity has been cut

Grammar

Modals

1 Note how modal verbs can be replaced by nouns, for example:

> They must be able to meet their energy needs.
> An ability to meet their energy needs is essential.

Which of these sentences is more formal?

Now transform the following sentences in a similar way using the word in brackets:

1 Everyone must save energy. (obligation) *Everyone has the obligation to save energy*
2 We don't need to build more power plants. (necessity) *There is no necessity*
3 We might be able to meet our energy requirements. (possibility) *There is a possibility of meeting our energy requirements*
4 The fact that coal can cause fatal diseases is often overlooked. (capacity) *The capacity of coal to cause ....*
5 Oil may well run out soon in certain producer countries. (probability)
  There is the probability that oil will run out ....

49

2 Note how modal verbs are often used with *there*, for example:

> There must be a reason for their decision.
> There could have been an accident.
> There might (well) be a need for further investigation.

The construction with *there* tends to be formal.

Now complete the following sentences with an appropriate *there* + modal
construction. Beware of the tenses!

1 We can't let this problem continue. _There must be_ a
   solution.

2 Why didn't they discover the causes? _They should've been_
   an investigation.

3 We can't be sure but _There might be_ another energy
   crisis soon.

4 If some countries conserve more energy,
   There should enough gas to last till the next century.

5 Conservation is a neglected issue. _There should be_
   more conservation campaigns.

6 If we are careful, _There will_ possibly _be_
   enough coal.

7 We've wasted a lot of time. _There should've been_ more
   research into solar energy in the 1950s and 1960s.

8 I don't know what everyone's worrying about.
   There must be a solution to these problems.

9 _There will be_ a war over energy before the end of
   this century.

10 That accident should never have happened.
   There should've been tighter safety measures.

3 Note how Gerund and Infinitive forms of modals can replace other
constructions:

> It's a shame that I have to leave now.→It's a shame **to have to** leave now.
> He was glad that he could help.→He was glad **of having been able to** help.

Rephrase the parts of the following sentences in italics with the form of
the modal indicated:

1 He was sorry *that he couldn't see them.* (Infinitive) _not to be able to see them_

2 He was afraid *that he would have to show his passport.* (Gerund) _of having to show_

3 He was angry *that he couldn't solve the problem.* (Gerund) _at not being able to solve the problem_

4 It's a pity *that we had to leave so soon.* (Infinitive) _to have had to leave so soon_

5 *As they can't help him*, they've sent him to the Tourist Office. (Gerund) _not being able to help him_

6 He regretted *that he hadn't been able to go.* (Gerund) _not having been able to go_

'I should put that cigarette out. I'm sure I can smell gas.'

Homework exercises   **(Recommended time: 1 hour)**

1 Read this typical Proficiency Directed Writing Composition exercise
and do as instructed below:

Projected opening of new coal power station causes protest and consternation in seaside tourist town

In the small seaside town of Nuttingdean much consternation was expressed last night when the local council announced

As a local hotel owner in Nuttingdean in the South of England, you are opposed to the building of a coal power station, even though you realise that new energy resources are needed. Write an angry letter of protest to your local council outlining the reasons for your objections and proposing alternatives.

---

1 Write a plan for the letter.
2 Write out a list of phrases of 'angry protest' that could be useful in the letter. Make sure that they are in an appropriate (formal) style for a letter to a local council.

2 Refer to pp.46–47 and plan and write two of the Directed Writing exercises you discussed there.

TEST   **COMPOSITION**   (Time: 1 hour)

Write this composition. Your answer must follow exactly the instructions given.

PUBLIC NOTICE

9 p.m. Tuesday, 23rd March

Town Hall, Braxbury

Mr Jeremy Walsh will talk on

'THE WASTE AND OVER-CONSUMPTION
OF ENERGY IN TODAY'S SOCIETY'

You attended this talk and were delighted by Mr Walsh's analyses of the causes of energy waste and proposals for energy conservation. Write Mr Walsh a letter congratulating him on his talk, explaining why you found it so good and suggesting that together you set up a conservation society and start a conservation campaign. (About 300 words, excluding your address, date, etc.)

8 The Technological Revolution

PAPER 3: USE OF ENGLISH

1 Wherever you go nowadays, you will see signs of the technological revolution – from computer games to electronic aids for the handicapped, from robot factories to the compact disc. And what about the compact disc? What do you know about it? Has it any advantages over the conventional record most of us still buy and play on our record-player?

2 Read this *Which?* article and then do the exercises.

What's Compact Disc?

It's a new kind of record-playing technology developed by Philips and Sony and launched in Britain in
5 1983. It has been described as the biggest breakthrough in home listening since stereo.

A Compact Disc (CD) – 12.5 cm in diameter – can have up to 70
10 minutes' playing time (equal to at least both sides of an ordinary LP) on one side only – the label is on the other side.

A CD player looks a bit like a hi-fi
15 cassette deck, though some are smaller. Instead of a stylus, a laser beam is used to play the disc.

In this report we refer to all ordinary black records as LPs.

20 How much does it cost?

Most players are about £450 to £650 at present; CDs cost about £10 to £13 depending on the record company.

25 What about existing records?

You can't play LPs on a CD player, and you can't play CDs on an ordinary record player. So if you went over to CD, you'd still need an
30 ordinary player or deck for your existing record collection. Many recordings currently on LP or cassette will be issued on CD as well, but it's most unlikely that all of them will be.

35 What's available?

There are about a dozen CD players in the shops now. Of the 200 or so discs around at the moment, over half are classical. Rock, jazz and pop
40 have been less well covered so far. Most major record companies who haven't yet released CDs will be doing so soon. Not all record shops stock CDs; shops selling players

COMPACT DISC
A SOUND REVOLUTION?

45 should be able to tell you which do.

At the moment most CDs are 'popular' titles: no problem if you want Beethoven's Fifth, James Last or Status Quo; tough luck if you're
50 after something more esoteric. Although other titles are being recorded all the time.

Is it easy to use?

Yes – about as easy as playing a
55 cassette. You open a small lid or compartment at the front of the player, pop the disc inside, close the lid and press *play*. An unsteady hand is no problem, and sticky fingermarks
60 can be wiped off the disc quite easily. You can *pause* a disc at any point and then restart it from there. There are other controls which aren't involved in basic playing.

65 What else is needed?

If you've got a hi-fi system with an amplifier or receiver which has an 'auxiliary' input socket – no problem: the CD player plugs into this. You
70 could probably use 'radio tuner' or 'tape playback' sockets instead if they're not already in use, but *not* an ordinary 'disc', 'phono' or 'pickup' input.

75 Connections apart, CD players should work with most stereo systems or music centres. But with a cheap system, you wouldn't get full value from CD's sound quality.
80 Some CD players will drive stereo headphones directly: a solo listener could manage with just these.

What are the advantages?

Apart from the sound quality:
85 ● no fiddly setting-up
● can give over an hour's unin-terrupted playing time (though on many discs it's less)
● resistant to jarring or vibration
90 ● player and disc quite small and neat
● simple basic operation – but lots of extra features possible
● CDs relatively durable and easy to
95 clean – should have indefinite life with reasonable care
● manufacturers can easily bring out models with remote control – like on a TV.

Any drawbacks?

100 Well, it's expensive and the range of music on CD is, at the moment, limited. Apart from this:
● it's very revealing of master re-
105 cordings that weren't very well en-gineered in the first place – with microphones in unsuitable positions, for example. A perfectionist might find this annoying. A few CDs are re-
110 issues of quite old and rather poor recordings.
● CD can have a very wide dynamic range – the difference between the loudest and quietest sounds that can
115 be reproduced. This adds to the realism, but listening to some CDs at home you could find that if you set the volume so that you can hear the softest passages, the loudest ones are
120 much too loud – and low-powered amplifiers could distort the sound.
● on some players it can take a while to find a point in the middle of long continuous works – shorter tracks
125 don't give this problem.
● CDs come in plastic boxes which are rather tricky to open and a bit fragile.
● player maintenance might work
130 out expensive – see below.

What about maintenance?

CD players have a lot of moving parts but it's too early to say whether these are likely to give trouble. The *laser* 135 won't last for ever – Sony reckon on three years' lifetime at three hours' use a day. Replacement cost could be around £75 (though of course diamond styli can also work out
140 expensive).

What about the future?

The worldwide adoption of a single technical standard (unlike video cas-settes or discs) and reports of heavy
145 demand over the first few months suggest that CD is here to stay. Though it's hard to say exactly what will happen, we don't think anyone with ordinary records and players
150 should panic – the huge number of these in existence means a continu-ing demand for years to come.
 Developments in CD over the next year or two are likely to bring more
155 and better discs, and players with extra features – such as a visual display of track titles or artists. There may also be smaller players for porta-ble or in-car use.

---

3 In pairs, try to work out *from the context* the meaning of the following words and phrases. Only look them up in a dictionary as a last resort!

1 launched (l.4)
2 went over to (ll.28–29)
3 currently (l.32)
4 around (at the moment) (l.38)
5 tough luck (l.49)
6 if you're after something more esoteric (ll.49–50)
7 pop (the disc inside) (l.57)
8 no fiddly setting-up (l.85)
9 resistant to jarring (l.89)
10 tricky to open (l.127)

4 **Jigsaw reading** Still in pairs, do the following exercise.

Student A reads the first half of the text and makes notes to answer these questions:

1 What is a compact disc?
2 How much does a compact disc system cost?
3 What's available on CD?
4 How easy is it to use a CD system?

Student B reads the second half of the text and makes notes to answer these questions:

1 What are the advantages of CD?
2 What drawbacks are there?
3 What maintenance is needed?
4 What does the future hold for CD?

When both have made notes, close your books and then ask each other the questions above, that is, Student B asks A the questions in the left-hand column, Student A asks B those in the right-hand column.

5 **Discussion**

In small groups, discuss each of the following and then report the opinions of the group to the rest of the class.

1 If the compact disc system catches on, what will some of the consequences be for the record industry, private collectors, radio, etc.?
2 What other major new breakthroughs can you think of in recent years in the media, transport, leisure, etc.? What effects have they had on people's lives?
3 Much has been written about the speed of change in the 20th century. Do *you* think things change too quickly?

Grammar

Passive constructions

1 Remember that the Passive can be used in all tenses and with modal verbs. Look at these examples from the Compact Disc text on pages 52–53.

A laser beam **is used** to play the disc.
Other titles **are being recorded** all the time.
It **has been described** as the biggest breakthrough in home listening since stereo.
. . . master recordings that **weren't very well engineered** in the first place.
Many recordings **will be issued** on CD . . .
Sticky fingermarks **can be wiped off** the disc quite easily.

Rephrase these sentences (in the Passive), beginning with the words given. Remember to provide all the relevant information which is given in the original sentence.

1 They have sold thousands of CD machines since 1983. (Thousands . . .)
2 A famous composer is conducting the concert tonight. (The concert tonight . . .)
3 Someone should have discovered that a long time ago. (That . . .)
4 They were demonstrating the new video system when I went there yesterday. (The new video system . . .)
5 Someone might find a solution to the problem soon. (A solution . . .)

2 Now study these Passive constructions, and then do the exercise:

I didn't hear my name called. / She didn't see her bag stolen.
He didn't feel his wallet (being) taken from his pocket.
I'd like this suit cleaned.
I'd like my car repaired/these photos developed/the house painted, etc.
She made her presence felt.
I found myself stranded on an island. / She found herself ignored by everyone.
He likes being admired. / I don't mind being criticised.
I like to be told what's going on.
I want to be left alone. / I don't want to be disturbed.
I'd like to be allowed to do the job myself.
It leaves much to be desired. / He was nowhere to be found.
You are to be congratulated.
There's a lot to do/to be done. / You are not to blame/to be blamed.
This house is to let/to be let; that house is to be sold.

Rephrase these sentences beginning with the words given. Again, remember to provide *all* the relevant information given in the original sentence.

1 I must congratulate you on passing your driving test. (You . . . .)
2 He is often criticised, but he doesn't seem to mind. (He . . .)
3 They're letting their house, not selling it. (Their . . .)
4 Her handbag was stolen, but she didn't see it happen. (She didn't . . .)
5 No one can blame you for what happened. (You are . . .)
6 I think the girl was knocked off her bicycle, but I didn't see it. (I didn't . . .)
7 They couldn't find the manager anywhere. (The manager . . .)
8 Please don't disturb me. (I don't want . . .)
9 The news was announced, but I didn't actually hear it myself. (I didn't . . .)
10 When he is asked about his past, he hates it. (He hates . . .)

Vocabulary

Nouns from phrasal verbs

1 Study each set of nouns on the left. Then cover them and fill in the blanks in the sentences with an appropriate noun from those given.

a)

onset	_Output_ at the factory increased by 50% last year.
outbreak	The _outcome_ of the meeting was most unexpected.
outburst	She owes her success to the _____ her parents gave her.
outcome	Right at the _outset_ I must say this information is confidential.
outlay	The _upkeep_ of the cathedral is very expensive.
output	There has been another _outbreak_ of fighting on the border.
outset	Our initial _outlay_ (to start the business) was £5,000.
upbringing	The _onset_ of the disease is marked by a fit of coughing.
upkeep	Suddenly there was an _outburst_ of laughter from the next room.

What other nouns do you know like this that begin with *in-*, *on-*, *out-* or *up-*?

b)

a breakdown	Let me give you a _rundown_ of what the manager said.
a break-in	One _drawback_ of the scheme is the very high cost. — *scolding*
a breakthrough	She gave the boy a _telling off_ for being so naughty.
a drawback	That young girl wears far too much _make-up_ for her age.
a giveaway	I'm sorry we're late, but we had a _breakdown_ on the way here.
a letdown	The impressionist did a _take-off_ of the Prime Minister.
make-up	It was a major _breakthrough_ in the field of telecommunications.
a rundown	After what I'd been led to expect, the concert was a _letdown_.
a take-off	He said he was poor, but his new shoes were a _giveaway_.
a telling-off	There was a _break-in_ at the office, but nothing was stolen.

What other nouns do you know like this that begin with *break-*, *let-*, *hold-*, *knock-* or *make-*?

2 Game: *Make up a story* (see Teacher's Guide Unit 8)

3 Rewriting sentences

One exercise in the Proficiency Paper 3 (Use of English) requires you to rewrite sentences using a word given, but the word is not to be altered in any way. Often the sentence will need a new structure. Study these examples, then rephrase the following sentences:

a) She told the boy off. (**telling-off**)
   She gave the boy a telling-off.
b) He broke down completely when he heard the news. (**breakdown**)
   He had/suffered a complete breakdown when he heard the news.

1 It cost them a lot of money to bring the boy up. (**upbringing**)

2 On average, people earn about £1,000 a year in that country. (**income**)

3 The long discussions finally resulted in nothing being done at all. (**outcome**)

4 Three houses in our street were broken into last week. (**break-ins**)

5 It is becoming very expensive to maintain this big house. (**upkeep**)

6 They reported to us in great detail what had happened. (**rundown**)

7 The restaurant was so disappointing that we never went back. (**letdown**)

8 When the war broke out, many people tried to escape across the border. (**outbreak**)

9 The amount the firm spent on the project initially was £15,000. (**outlay**)

10 What gave her away in the end was her distinctive handwriting. (**giveaway**)

Answering questions on a passage

In Section B of the Proficiency Paper 3 (Use of English), you will have to read a passage and then answer questions on it and write a summary.

There are normally two kinds of question: 1 'Explain the phrase . . .', and 2 'How/What/Why/In what way/etc. . . .' type questions.

1   Read this passage carefully and be prepared to give a general idea of what it is about. Then read the notes and examples opposite and do the exercises.

They have you taped – and there aren't enough safeguards

The dangers of increasing computerization of personal, official and business information have long been recognized, and are
5   scarcely any longer controversial. First, data can be stored which is inaccurate, incomplete or irrelevant, and yet can be used as the basis for important decisions
10   affecting people's lives.

Second, people may have no idea of the information kept on them, have no way of finding out, and no opportunity to correct mistakes.
15   Third, there is the possibility that the information can fall into unauthorized hands, who could use it for all sorts of hostile, even criminal, purposes. Fourth, the informa-
20   tion could be used for a purpose other than that for which it was gathered. Fifth, because computer systems can now communicate with each other easily and speedily,
25   the possibility is increased that comprehensive Big Brother files will be compiled on private citizens.

From birth to death, every individual will regularly find some-
30   thing about him appearing in some file or other. Estimates of how many different files are kept on the average adult individual range from 15 to 50. Some may be
35   thought trivial in themselves — though even library computers can now reveal that a reader took out

a book on guerrilla warfare and another on Marxist ideology.
40   Credit card files might disclose an inappropriate spending pattern. The Vehicle Licensing Department keeps tabs on every driver's change of address, and their computer is
45   available to the police. The list of information kept on the individual — his health, income, social security position, details of his property, his car, his job, and so on — goes
50   on.

Of course, for those who have been in trouble with the police, or been members of an 'undesirable' political group, even though they
55   have done nothing illegal, the information kept on them multiplies. More and more of all this information has been removed from the old-fashioned filing cabinet and is
60   being put into computers.

The need for safeguards is not limited to personal information.

Business, too, needs protection. If a company's list of customers, or its
65   pricing or production formulae, got into the hands of competitors, the result could be financial ruin.

In 1978, The Lindop Committee set out the principles which should
70   govern data protection: (1) The individual should know what personal data is being kept, why it is needed, how long it will be used, who will use it, for what purpose,
75   and for how long. (2) Personal data should be handled only to the extent and for the purposes made known at the outset, or authorized subsequently. (3) It should be accu-
80   rate and complete, and relevant and timely for the purpose for which it is used. (4) No more data should be handled than is necessary for the purposes made known. (5)
85   The individual should be able to verify that those principles have been complied with.

2 When you have to 'explain a phrase', you may have to work out what it means from the context, so read the sentence in which it occurs *and* the sentences before and after for clues. Your written explanation should be brief. Look at these examples and then do the rest:

Explain (in other words) the phrase . . .

1 'scarcely any longer controversial' (l.5)
2 'fall into unauthorized hands' (ll.16–17)
3 'comprehensive Big Brother files' (l.26)
4 'trivial in themselves' (l.35)
5 'inappropriate spending pattern' (l.41)
6 'keeps tabs on' (l.43)
7 'the old-fashioned filing cabinet' (ll.58–59)
8 'got into the hands of' (l.66)
9 'authorized subsequently' (ll.78–79)
10 'complied with' (l.87)

Possible explanations . . .

1 hardly likely to cause much discussion or argument any more
2 be seen, or be obtained, by people without authority or permission
3 complete, thorough files on every individual (as described by George Orwell in his novel '1984')

NOTE: Your explanations must of course explain the phrase as used in the passage.

---

3 Most of the questions on the passage fall into the 'What . . .?/ Why . . .?/In what way(s) . . .?/How . . .?' category. Read each question carefully, find the sentence or paragraph in the passage to which it refers, and then decide how best to answer it. You do not need to write long sentences which, for example, repeat the question. Read the questions below and the suggested answers to the first three, then answer the rest individually:

1 In what ways can the storing of inaccurate information be dangerous?
   (Because important but wrong decisions can be made based on such information.)
2 What is one of the biggest fears about personal data on computer?
   (The information could be used for criminal purposes.)
3 How could 'comprehensive Big Brother files' be compiled on private citizens?
   (Computer systems can now easily communicate information to each other.)
4 What details are likely to be filed about an individual?
5 Why is there more information about certain people than others?
6 Why do business firms also need data protection?
7 What do you think the Lindop Committee was set up to do?
8 What did the Committee suggest the individual should know about his or her personal data on computer?

Now compare your answers with a partner.

Homework exercise

(Recommended time: 40 minutes)

Summary

Summarise in about 100 words what the article opposite says are the dangers of increasing computerisation of personal and other information, and what the principles are which should govern the protection of computerised information.

TEST   **USE OF ENGLISH**   (Time: 1 hour 15 minutes)

SECTION A

1   *Finish each of the following sentences in such a way that it means exactly the same as the sentence before it.*

EXAMPLE: They wrote the first report three years ago.
ANSWER: The first report *was written three years ago.*

a) You will only be able to find the answers when you have read the report in detail.
    Only *when you have read the report in detail will you be able to find the answers.*

b) The technological revolution is opening up a whole new world, but many people are worried by it.
    In spite of *the fact that the ... a whole new world opened by the technological revolution*

c) He was annoyed that he had to go back to his office in the evening.
    He was annoyed at *having go back to his office ...*

d) The boy became so confused and worried that he left home.
    So *worried & confused was the boy that he ...*

e) Since I've never seen or heard a compact disc, I can't comment on it.
    Never *having seen or heard a compact disc, ...*

f) When I heard the telephone ring, I answered it immediately.
    On *hearing the telephone ring, ...*

g) I found the article about data protection very interesting.
    I was *very interested in the article about ...*

h) The record companies are challenging the claims made by the manufacturers.
    The claims *are being challenged by the ...*

i) The new computer was being demonstrated while I was there, but I didn't see it.
    I didn't *see the computer being ...*

j) We must all do a great deal before we move house.
    There is *a great deal to do before we move house*

2   *For each of the sentences below, write a new sentence as similar as possible in meaning to the original sentence, but using the words given: these words must not be altered in any way.*

EXAMPLE: What happened is not your fault. (**blame**)
ANSWER: *You are not to blame for what happened.*

a) Wherever she goes, she always acts in such a way that other people know she is there. (**presence**)
b) We must be able to solve this problem. (**solution**)
c) There is little point in even considering the other theories. (**worth**)
d) He's a much more careful worker these days. (**carefully**)
e) We can only wait and see what happens. (**choice**)
f) I'm sorry I didn't write to you last month. (**apologise**)
g) They might have got lost. (**possibility**)
h) We have spent a considerable amount of money on this project. (**outlay**)
i) The comedian imitated the Prime Minister in his stage act. (**take-off**)
j) I would like to complain most strongly about the play which was performed at your theatre last week. (**complaint**)

SECTION B

3 Read the following passage, then answer the questions which follow it.

The last days of my childhood were also the last days of the village. I belonged to that generation which saw, by chance, the end of a thousand years' life. The change came late to our Cotswold
5 valley, didn't really show itself till the late 1920s; I was twelve by then, but during that handful of years I witnessed the whole thing happen.

Myself, my family, my generation, were born in a world of silence; a world of hard work and
10 necessary patience, of backs bent to the ground, hands massaging the crops, of waiting on weather and growth; of villages like ships in the empty landscapes and the long walking distances between them; of white narrow roads, rutted by
15 hooves and cartwheels, innocent of oil or petrol, down which people passed rarely, and almost never for pleasure, and the horse was the fastest thing moving. Man and horse were all the power we had – abetted by levers and pulleys. But the
20 horse was king, and almost everything grew around him: fodder, smithies, stables, paddocks, distances, and the rhythm of our days. His eight miles an hour was the limit of our movements, as it had been since the days of the Romans. That
25 eight miles an hour was life and death, the size of our world, our prison.

This was what we were born to, and all we knew at first. Then, to the scream of the horse, the change began. The brass-lamped motor-car
30 came coughing up the road, followed by the clamorous charabanc; the solid-tyred bus climbed the dusty hills and more people came and went. Chickens and dogs were the early sacrifices, falling demented beneath the wheels.

The old folk, too, had strokes and seizures, faced 35 by speeds beyond comprehension. Then scarlet motor-bikes, the size of five-barred gates, began to appear in the village, on which our youths roared like rockets up the two-minute hills, then spent weeks making repairs and adjustments. 40

These appearances did not immediately alter our lives; the cars were freaks and rarely seen, the motor-bikes mostly in pieces, we used the charabancs only once a year, and our buses at first were experiments. Meanwhile Lew Ayres, 45 wearing a bowler-hat, ran his wagonette to Stroud twice a week. The carriage held six, and the fare was twopence, but most people preferred to walk. Mr West, from Sheepscombe, ran a cart every day, and would carry your parcels for 50 a penny. But most of us still did the journey on foot, heads down to the wet Welsh winds, ignoring the carters – whom we thought extortionate – and spending a long hard day at our shopping. 55

But the car-shying horses with their rolling eyes gave signs of the hysteria to come. Soon the village would break, dissolve, and scatter, become no more than a place for pensioners. It had a few years left, the last of its thousand, and they 60 passed almost without our knowing. They passed quickly, painlessly, in motor-bike jaunts, in the shadows of the new picture-palace, in quick trips to Gloucester (once a foreign city) to gape at the jazzy shops. Yet right to the end, like the false 65 strength that precedes death, the old life seemed as lusty as ever.

a) What happened to the village during the author's childhood?
b) Why was it a 'world of silence' that the author was born into?
c) Explain in other words the phrase 'hands massaging the crops' (l.11).
d) Why was the horse described as 'king' when the author was a child?
e) Explain the phrase 'the limit of our movements' (l.23).
f) What initial effects did the motor car have on village life?
g) Explain the phrase 'the early sacrifices' (ll.33–34).
h) Why do you think the author described the motor-bikes as 'the size of five-barred gates' (l.37)?
i) Why didn't the appearance of motor vehicles immediately change their lives?
j) Why did most of the villagers continue to ignore the services of Lew Ayres and Mr West?
k) What does the author mean by 'the hysteria to come' (l.57).
l) Summarise in 50–100 words what the passage says about the effects of the advent of the motor car on the life of the village in which the author was brought up.

9 Personal Experiences

1 Listening

The phrase to 'drop a brick' means 'to make a foolish remark which hurts someone's feelings and which usually causes acute embarrassment to the speaker'. Listen to the short anecdote and then answer these questions:

1 Where was the speaker at the time?
2 What was the woman doing? Where?
3 Who was the speaker sitting next to?
4 What do you think the speaker actually said to the man?
5 Why did the speaker begin to blush?
6 How did he try to explain himself?
7 What did the other man say in reply? And how did he say it?
8 How did the speaker feel? Why?

Have you ever been in a situation like the one the speaker described? If so, how did you feel? Why? What happened?

2 Reading and predicting (before listening)

There are times in life when we have no idea what we might hear – when turning on the radio just to see what's on, for example, or walking into a shop or a restaurant. In such situations, our own language competence allows us (usually) very quickly to gather what is happening and what is being said. There are many occasions, however, on which we are prepared for what we will hear, for example when we turn on the radio to listen to the news, a play, a talk, or go to a live lecture or debate. Because we know the title (e.g. a talk on '18th-century English drinking glasses' or a debate on 'Conservation in the 1990s'), or because we know what kind of language to expect (e.g. with radio news), we can already predict the kinds of things people will say. And indeed, if we attend a lecture, we may already have specific questions in our mind which we hope or expect will be answered.

A Listening Comprehension exercise is rather like this. If you look at the task carefully, it will not only give you the questions to which you want answers, it will also tell you a lot about what you are going to hear.

First passage

You are going to listen to an anecdote told by a woman, but before you listen, read the four multiple-choice questions carefully.

a) In pairs, work out what the questions are to which you want answers. For example, Question 1 will be: 'What did the woman know about the man *for a fact*?' (NOT What did she assume about the man?)
b) With your partner, try to predict some of the contents of the anecdote.

1 Although the woman couldn't remember the man's name, she knew for a fact that

   A he worked on a national magazine.
   B he annoyed a lot of people.
   C he was a famous person.
   D he had organised the charity party.

2 While they chatted, the man

   A showed that he knew a lot about the woman.
   B asked if the woman would like to meet his wife.
   C told the woman he always read the magazine.
   D gave the woman the story of his life.

3 When the man told the woman about his travels,

   A she became very interested.
   B she wanted to know a lot more.
   C she was even more mystified.
   D she began to feel ill.

4 The woman only remembered who the man was

   A when she recalled the interview.
   B after someone had pointed out his wife.
   C when she was collecting her coat.
   D when she had gone into the Ladies' Room.

3 Now listen to the anecdote and answer the multiple-choice questions.

4 Discuss your answers. How accurate were your predictions?

5 **Second passage**

Now listen to part of a radio programme about how people deal with disaster. Follow the same procedure as you did for the first passage. Read the multiple-choice items first, decide what questions you want answered, what the extract will be about, etc.

1 John and his wife

   A sailed the Caribbean for six years.
   B went to the island of Antigua in 1982.
   C bought their boat ten weeks before they left.
   D were shipwrecked off the coast of Spain.

2 When they got back to England, John

   A forgot about the West Indies.
   B found everyday life unexciting.
   C drifted around doing nothing.
   D steered clear of his office.

3 What was forecast for the voyage?

   A A hurricane-force gale.
   B Fine, clear weather.
   C Strong winds.
   D A very heavy storm.

4 From the way John described the event, it was clear that he had been

   A absolutely terrified.
   B crushed by a large wave.
   C swept off the deck of the boat.
   D impressed by the experience.

6 Now discuss your answers.

Grammar

News items on radio and television tend to employ a great deal of Reported Speech, and there is a certain formality in the language used generally in reporting news. This section looks at aspects of formal reporting.

 You are going to hear a radio news item. When you have heard it, answer these questions:

1 What was it about? Do you remember any details?
2 What did you notice about the language? Was it very formal? Can you give any examples?

Some formal ways of reporting speech

1 Look at these two sentence patterns commonly used when reporting news. They occurred in the item you heard above. Can you remember the rest of the sentences?

> Speaking at the headquarters . . ., a spokesman declared that the figures were . . .
> (= When he was speaking . . .)

> When (he was) asked ⎫
> On being asked   ⎬ about the possibility . . ., he replied that it was . . .
> Asked   ⎭

2 Look at the variety of verbs we use when reporting what people said. You are going to hear journalists interviewing people in preparation for news items or stories. Listen to the interviews, and after each one report what was asked and what the answers were. Use language from the box below.

(On being)	asked (for information) about . . .,
	questioned about . . .,
	invited to comment on . . .,
	accused of (doing) . . .,
	requested (to do) . . .,
(When)	pressed for information about . . .,
	told/informed that . . .,
	interviewed about . . .,

	told reporters/said (that) . . .
	stated/declared (that) . . .
the pop star	replied (that) . . .
	felt/thought/believed (that) . . .
the spokesman	accepted/agreed (that) . . .
	acknowledged/conceded (that) . . .
the police sergeant	denied ⎫ (doing)/(that) . . .
	admitted ⎭
	confessed (that)/to (doing) . . .
	doubted/wondered whether . . .

3 Listen to the interviews again and extract the main points from each. Where necessary, write down exactly what the people said. Then write the reports as news items for homework.

4 Formal and informal reporting verbs

There are many verbs one can use in English in place of *say, tell, ask,* etc. Note those which would be used in more formal reporting and rarely in everyday speech:

Verbs commonly used to report speech in an informal/neutral style:	say, tell, ask, want to know, wonder, answer
Verbs commonly used to report speech in a formal style:	state, declare, recount, enquire, ask oneself, reply

Read these short passages, then report what was said. Report 1 with informal reporting verbs, and 2 with more formal reporting verbs.

1 'Why were you so disappointed?' asked John. 'Well,' said Mary, 'when we booked the tickets, we thought the seats were in the front row.' 'Didn't you ask at the box office?' asked John. 'No,' said Mary.

2 'Where were you on the night of the 13th?' the Judge asked. 'I don't know,' said the witness. 'I can't remember.' Then the Judge asked: 'Have you tried to remember?' 'Of course,' said the witness, 'but it's a blank.'

5 Other constructions for reporting speech

Often we report what people say or said by using some other verb construction. Look at these examples:

'Congratulations on passing the exam.'→I **congratulated** her **on passing** the exam.
'You've done a good job.'————————→She **complimented** me **on doing** a good job.
'I'll be there early.' ————————→He **promised to be** there early.

Here are other verbs we use in this way: *doubt, suggest, regret, threaten, apologise.* How many more can you think of? Make a list, then compare with a partner.

Now report what these people said using verbs like those above:

1 'I'd go and ask that man if I were you,' she said to me.
2 'Don't touch that hot iron!' she said to the boy.
3 'Thank you very much for helping me,' he said to her.
4 'Yes, I committed the robbery,' the man said in court.
5 'Go on,' he said to them. 'Eat it! You'll enjoy it.'

Vocabulary

1 There are many verbs we can use instead of *say, tell* or *ask* to indicate moods and attitudes. Read this and say what the reporting verbs imply.

'Don't do that again!' he *snapped*. 'I'm rapidly losing my temper.' Then he turned and *bawled* up the stairs, 'When are you kids coming down for breakfast?!' He *muttered* something about being left to do everything while Jane was out at work, and went back to the kitchen. 'Why is it impossible to get kids to do washing-up?' he *groaned*, and went back to frying the bacon.

Apart from the words the man spoke, how do you know what sort of mood he was in?

How many more verbs can you add to this list to show the moods or attitudes of speakers when reporting what they say?
whisper, hiss, shout, snap, call (out), stammer, mumble, . . .

2   Adjectives used when reporting impressions, emotions and feelings

1   Look at these adjectives. Which would you use to
describe the faces?

pleased, glad, satisfied, excited, enthralled, thrilled, delighted
puzzled, mystified, confused, baffled
bored, fed up, depressed, low (*inf.*), browned off (*inf.*), discontented (*formal*)
interested, curious, fascinated, intrigued
worried, anxious, concerned, apprehensive, frightened, horrified, terrified
irritated, impatient, annoyed, exasperated, infuriated, angry, furious, indignant
surprised, astonished, amazed, stunned, staggered, astounded
embarrassed, disconcerted, humiliated
disappointed, disillusioned

How pleased does he or she look? Just 'glad'? Or
'absolutely thrilled'?

2   Look at these adjectives and discuss with a partner what kinds of
things you find exciting, worrying, exasperating, etc. For example,
I always find waiting in queues absolutely exasperating.

		!	!!	!!!
pleasing	satisfying		exciting, enthralling	thrilling, exhilarating
puzzling	mystifying		confusing	baffling
boring	depressing			
interesting	fascinating		intriguing	
worrying	frightening		horrifying	terrifying
irritating	annoying		exasperating	infuriating
surprising	astonishing		amazing	staggering, astounding
embarrassing	disconcerting		humiliating	

3   In pairs or small groups, tell each other about any experience you
have had which was humorous, embarrassing, intriguing, frightening,
etc. Begin like this:
     (I think) the most /embarrassing/ experience I've ever had was when . . .
or (I think the most /frightening/ thing that's every happened to me was when . . .
or I don't think I've ever been so /humiliated/ as I was when . . .
or I'll never forget the time I (did . . .). It was so /exciting/.

Then continue to ask and/or say:
  – where you were, and who with (if others were present);
  – how it all started – what you were doing, or going to do;
  – what happened first – and then? – and after that? etc.;
  – what you (or others) said (if anything); etc.

Homework exercises

(Recommended time: 1 hour 30 minutes)

1 Finish each of the following sentences in such a way that it means exactly the same as the sentence printed before it.

1 'I think that you've drawn up some excellent plans. I must congratulate you.'
'I must congratulate _you on drawing up .... or on having drawn up_

2 The manager confessed to being astounded when they told him about the robbery.
On _hearing the ... being told about robbery the manager confessed to being_

3 She found the whole proceedings thoroughly embarrassing.
She was _thoroughly embarrassed by the whole proceedings._

4 'If I were you,' he said, 'I'd go and speak to your bank manager.'
He advised _..._

5 'By next January I shall have been here for twenty years,' he told us.
He told us that _..._

6 So concerned were they about their son that they took him to a specialist.
They _were so concerned about ..._

7 Since she couldn't get through to the police, she ran next door for help.
Not _being able to get through to the police_

8 I set my alarm carefully because I had to get up especially early.
Having _... I set my alarm carefully to get up especially early_

9 'I'm extremely sorry I couldn't come to the meeting.'
'I must apologise _for not being able to come_

10 The way he kept clicking his fingers was very irritating.
I was _very irritated by the way he kept clicking._

2 Fill in the blanks in this passage with *one* suitable word.

Tom was so _upset_ (1) at being made redundant at his age that he seriously _considered_ (2) whether he would ever be able to get another job again. On _being_ (3) told by the Personnel Manager that his services _would_ (4) no longer be required, he was at first _astoun_ (5). He really couldn't understand it. What had he done to make them sack him? But then he became _annoyed_ (6), almost angry. 'How dare they?' was what he thought. And it was after that initial anger that the depression had set in. When _asked_ (7) by any of the family or his friends what he was _going_ (8) to do, he answered with a simple 'I don't know', and the _way_ (9) he said it was enough to warn anyone _off_ (10) making any further enquiries. He _thought_ (11) at one point of starting his own business, but _having_ (12) been employed all his life by someone else, he didn't know where to start. On another occasion, _talking_ (13) to others who had been made redundant, he suggested they _could_ (14) start something called a 'co-operative' which he had heard about, but nothing came of that, either.
It was while he was walking by the river one day that he had an idea so _brilliant_ (15) that it was to change the course of his life.

3 Composition

Plan and write a composition (about 350 words) giving an account of an experience you will never forget.

65

TEST   LISTENING COMPREHENSION   (Time: approx. 30 minutes)

PART 1

For each of questions 1–5 put a tick in one of the boxes A, B, C or D.

1 The speaker didn't quite know how to describe his experience because

A he couldn't remember all the details.

B it was so embarrassing.

C he had never told the story before.

D it was so strange.

A
B
C
D

2 When the speaker spotted the hitchhiker,

A his first thought was to drive on past.

B he recognised him immediately.

C he could see the man was surrounded by mist.

D he was driving to a business meeting in the north.

A
B
C
D

3 The speaker stopped for the hitchhiker because

A he was a business colleague of his.

B he knew the man slightly.

C the man was holding a card with the name of the village on it.

D he knew the man's car had broken down.

A
B
C
D

4 The speaker dropped the man

A outside Winchester.

B 20 miles from his home.

C at the end of his road.

D near the telephone box.

A
B
C
D

5 What had happened earlier that evening?

A The speaker's wife had had a call from John.

B John had come to the speaker's house for an hour.

C John's wife had been to see the speaker's wife.

D John had died in a very bad car crash.

A
B
C
D

PART 2

For questions 6–15, listen and fill in the missing information.

6 Most of the work in the Colchester factory is done by ....

7 How long does it take to produce finished components now? ....

8 And how many men are needed? ....

9 It used to take .... to produce finished components.

10 And how many men were needed? ....

11 What does the Fanuc plant produce in a month? ....

12 How many men look after the night shift at Fanuc? ....

13 The Government grant received by the Colchester plant was ....

14 How much money has the Department of Industry set aside for FMS? ....

15 The Rolls-Royce plant has increased its productivity by ....

PART 3

For each of questions 16–18 put a tick in one of the boxes A, B, C or D.

16 Traffic came to a standstill in Oakton because

A there was a police rally in the town.

B the river near the town overflowed into the centre.

C there was a massive amount of cars in the centre of the town.

D there was a large crowd demanding a new by-pass.

A
B
C
D

17 What has happened in the past ten years?

A The population has grown by 7,000.

B Plans for the new road have constantly been postponed.

C Some of the very old buildings have fallen down.

D The town has become an extremely popular holiday resort.

A
B
C
D

18 When interviewed, Ray Griffiths was

A extremely apprehensive.

B very depressed.

C exasperated.

D utterly amazed.

A
B
C
D

10 Mind over Matter

PAPER 5: **INTERVIEW**

1 In small groups, discuss these questions:

1 If you are ill, is it possible to 'think yourself better' (that is, without going to a doctor or taking any medicine)?
2 Do you know or have you read of anyone who has had dental treatment or undergone an operation under hypnosis?
3 You have probably read about people in certain parts of the world who can walk on fire, lie on a bed of nails, pass daggers, swords or skewers through parts of their body, survive for long periods near naked in extreme cold, or even levitate themselves. What do you think about such reports? Do you believe them, or are you sceptical?

2 Study photo A opposite and in pairs ask and answer these questions. Remember the language you practised in Unit 5 to ask for a repetition, express assumptions, etc.

About the photo

1 Where would you say this photo was taken? Why?
2 What is the man doing (or what does it look as if he's doing)?
3 What is the reaction of the onlookers (or what do you think they're thinking)?
4 Do you think the man is really levitating, or is it a trick or illusion of some kind? If you suspect that there is some trickery, how do you think it is done? If you think the man is really levitating, why do you believe it?

Personal

1 If you were ever actually present when someone did this, would you be able to believe your eyes?
2 What is the most unusual thing you have ever seen anyone do? Tell me about it.

For general discussion

1 It is said that 'the camera never lies'? What do you think?
2 Why are many scientists so sceptical of phenomena like levitation, metal-bending (Yuri Geller and others), the levitation and movement of objects (psychokinesis), and so on?
3 If you were given the opportunity to have an operation under hypnosis (even, for example, to have a tooth taken out), would you take it? Why?/Why not?

3 Now study photo B opposite and write down a number of questions about it to ask another student. Remember to write questions about the photo, personal questions, and more general questions for discussion on related topics.
Ask each other your questions in pairs.

Read and discuss

1 This is an edited version of an article which appeared in *Woman*, a British women's magazine, in 1975. Read this introduction.

Repeat to yourself the phrase: 'My hands are warm' every 20 seconds or so, and they will feel warm! You'll feel warm enough to imagine yourself basking on a broiling hot beach.

If you repeat to yourself the phrase: 'I feel quite quiet' every 20 seconds, you will feel a calmness steal over you.

In a different context, these phrases and others like them, phrases which tell the body what is expected of it, are helping patients to help themselves.

Scientists and doctors are discovering surprising new ways of looking at health. One recurring theme is that we need to be nudged towards the realisation that we have within us a great, untapped potential responsible for maintaining good health.

Close your eyes and imagine that if there were no medicines, hospitals, clinics, medical staff, how you would work a cure by yourself?

If you find it hard to list suggestions perhaps, like me, you have come to regard medical care as necessary as food and fresh air. No doubt the mechanics of medicine are *vital*, but perhaps alongside the existing professionals we need a new breed of experts specifically to bring out the best in us.

What suggestions can you make in answer to the question: 'If there were no medicines, hospitals, clinics or medical staff, how would you cure yourself?'

2 Jigsaw reading

Now, in small groups, each read **one** of the following extracts from the article (a, b, c or d), work out or look up in a dictionary any important new vocabulary, and then report what it says to the rest of the group.

3 As training for the discussion part of the Proficiency Interview, discuss this statement: 'The power of mind over matter, the power to think yourself well (or ill), is a power we all possess, but seem to have forgotten in the twentieth century.'

a)

Control your body

Self-control of a remarkable kind is being taught by doctors in Topeka, Kansas. Dr. Elmar Green and his wife Alyce, both psychologists, set out in 1964 to discover what a person could do to change his or her own physiological state. The method they employed is autogenic training (i.e. a process that takes place at a conscious level).

The doctors launched a two-week training programme with 33 housewives, whose first lesson was to warm their hands at will. With practice they mastered an increase of up to 10 degrees Fahrenheit, not for the purpose of making cold hands warm, but to alter the patterns of the brain.

Today this exercise has particular significance for the migraine victim, who can learn to control the temperature of her hands as a step in gaining voluntary relief from headache.

Epileptics learn similar controls so that they can spare themselves an oncoming epileptic brain pattern.

The Kansas doctors would describe a homely old thermometer as a 'biofeedback instrument': it feeds back biological information to the patient about herself. The whole point of 'biofeedback' is that it makes it possible to know consciously what normally carries on at a sub-conscious level; i.e. heart beat, rhythm of breathing.

In time, no laboratory instrument is required. The patient becomes so attuned to the rhythm of her brainwaves, or patterns, that she can change them at will.

Most people can learn the technique in 15-minute sessions over a couple of days. Awareness is the key factor.

Not long ago I went to the outpatient department of a London teaching hospital with a painful splinter under my nail. When, finally, the doctor got it removed, I asked how painful the nail would be that evening, he answered: 'It'll be as painful as you think it's going to be.'

b)

The body heals itself

Pointers from biologist Lyall Watson: 'Yogis, with their super-control, can push skewers through their cheeks without pain, without blood, without infection.

'Pain is a warning device designed to tell us what is wrong. Once you know what is wrong, you can cancel out the pain. Anyone determined can learn to control, even without a feedback instrument.

'You can learn to make one finger cold, one hand hot. You control the temperature of the skin by the amount of blood you allow to reach the surface layers.'

Scientists are making a study of faith healers in an attempt to find out what takes place when a patient puts him or herself in the hands of the untrained. It is a subject that has remained a mystery since biblical times, but Dr. Watson is convinced of one thing:

'Whether you're in the hands of a medical doctor or a faith healer, you, the patient, help the healer. The body should know what is wrong and put it right. By the time symptoms can be detected, the disease has progressed. The body knows about it before that stage.'

c)

The magic touch of a loving hand

Someone else who credits the body with being in charge is an American Franciscan, Sister Justa Smith, who combines her vocation with a scientific career.

She says: 'There is something within the body that controls healing. It isn't by knowledge that it happens. Doctors do many things to assist the healing process, but the body heals by itself.'

She smiled: 'We should be able to heal not only ourselves but each other. *We can make each other ill!*'

Responsibility, then, is not only the responsibility to keep ourselves well, but an awareness of how we are affecting our loved ones, colleagues and friends.

Said Sister Justa: 'The ability to heal is almost innate in human beings. You see it particularly in young mums when they immediately put their hand on the spot—the grazed knee, the bumped elbow—that is causing a small child to cry. The magical touch of a loving hand is all that is required.

'When someone isn't well,' she continued, 'we put our hand on their head. Women, in particular, do it almost automatically. Somehow we touch them and perhaps it is through this sense of touch that we dispense our healing talents.'

d)

Emotional control – a cure for cancer?

Take a deep breath, and as you blow out, mentally say 'relax'. Think of the muscles round your eyes. Relax them. Think of your jaw: open your mouth wide and allow it to fall to the most relaxed position. Take a deep breath, and as you blow it out, mentally say 'relax' to yourself . . .

These exercises are not from a new beauty bible but are part of a series put on tape by Dr. Carl Simonton, an American radiation therapy specialist who regards the patient's emotional considerations to be highly significant in the treatment of cancer.

In his practice, the radiation treatment is backed up with a course in awareness. It is a purely psycho-logical therapy.

Said Dr. Simonton: 'Anyone involved in the treatment of cancer becomes aware of the great differences between patients, and the personality, including its emotional stresses are features of the development of the disease and its progress.

'I believe that the biggest feature precipitating the disease is the loss of a significant object—a loved one, or maybe a job. It can be a real or imagined loss, but what matters is the patient's response to it. Very often a feeling of helplessness and hopelessness overtakes them. Many men experience an onset of the disease within a year of retiring.'

What a patient believes about his treatment is vital. Dr. Simonton considers that his own belief system plays an integral part in his patients' response: his attitude affects them.

In Britain, the British Cancer Council is helping nurses and medical students to take an optimistic view. After all, he says, 30,000 cures were effected here in one year, and the figure could have been doubled had fear not stopped patients getting help early.

Patient power is more potent than we realised, and perhaps it is time to look inside ourselves for the strength we need to maintain good health and to help one another.

Grammar

Variations on standard *if*-clauses

1 Study this and then do the exercise (**2**) below.

1 Some standard types.   Some variations

a)	If you do this, you'll get better. ⟶ Do this, and you'll get better.
	If you don't concentrate, you'll never do it. ⟶ Concentrate, or/otherwise you'll never do it.
	If you are (*or* should be) interested, ⟶ Should you be interested, I can lend you a
	I can lend you a good book about it. good book about it.
b)	If it weren't for the rain, we would go out. ⟶ Were it not for the rain/But for the rain,
	we would go out.
	If it weren't for the fact that it's so ⟶ Were it not for the fact that it's so
	fantastic, I would believe it. fantastic, I would believe it.
c)	If I had been there, I would have wanted ⟶ Had I been there, I would have wanted
	more proof. more proof.
	If it hadn't been for the rain, we would ⟶ Had it not been for the rain/ But for the
	have gone out. rain, we would have gone out.

2 Remember these words to introduce *if-* clauses:

even if	Some people will believe even if they don't see it themselves.
provided ⎫ providing ⎭	You can do it too ⎰ provided ⎱ (that) you concentrate. ⎱ providing ⎰
on condition (that)	I'll show you the photographs on condition (that) you don't show them to anyone else. (=on one condition, and that condition is . . .)
suppose ⎫ supposing ⎭	Suppose ⎫ (that) ⎰ you are ill, what will you do then? Supposing ⎭ ⎱ you were lost, how would you find your way home? you had been there, would you have believed it?
as/so long as	You can borrow my camera ⎰ so long as ⎱ you promise to look after it. ⎱ as long as ⎰

3 *If only* . . . and *I wish* . . . for regrets:

If only more people could do that! (I wish more people could do that!) If only he had taken some photos! (I wish he had taken some photos!)	(=If more people could do that, it would be good.) (=If he had taken some photos, it would have been useful/good.)

2 Finish each of the following sentences in such a way that it means exactly the same as the sentence printed before it.

1 What would *you* do if you could heal people like that. (Supposing . . .)
2 I would never have believed it if I hadn't seen it with my own eyes. (Had . . .)
3 If it hadn't been for the faith healer, she would never have lived. (But . . .)
4 If you don't believe in it, you'll never be able to do it. (Believe . . .)
5 If you want to know more, I can tell you who to write to. (Should . . .)
6 I wish I could believe in mind over matter. (If . . .)
7 What would you have thought if you had seen the fakir pour water round the tent? (Suppose . . .)
8 Please telephone us if you require any further information. (Should . . .)
9 I'll show you the photos if you promise not to laugh. (As long as . . .)
10 You can do it if you think positively. (Providing . . .)

Vocabulary

Related nouns and verbs

1 Many nouns in English have the same (or almost the same) form as the verb with which they are related. Sometimes they *are* the same in form, spelling and pronunciation (e.g. con'trol/to con'trol). Sometimes they have the same pronunciation, but are spelt differently (e.g. 'practice/to 'practise, a 'licence/to 'license, etc.). Sometimes, however, they are spelt the same, but are pronounced differently. Study the words on the left, noting the main stress. Then cover them and read aloud the sentences on the right. (The sentences are not necessarily good English style, but they *are* good for your reading!)

Noun	Verb	
a 'record	to re'cord	This is a record which she recorded last year.
a 'present	to pre'sent	He presented me with a present.
a 'contract	to con'tract	Please sign this contract. / She's contracted measles.
a 'contrast	to con'trast	What a contrast in the weather. / Contrast this with that.
a 'discount	to dis'count	You can discount the discount.
a 'conflict	to con'flict	There are conflicting reports of the conflict.
a 'convict	to con'vict	The convict was convicted of murder.
an 'object	to ob'ject	I object to the object of the exercise.
a 'permit	to per'mit	They won't permit you to do that without a permit.
a 'suspect	to su'spect	The suspect was suspected of having broken the window.
a 'subject	to sub'ject	The subject was subjected to examination by the committee.
a 'project	to pro'ject	The project we were on was projected for 1990.
'progress	to pro'gress	Progress is slow, but we're progressing!
'produce	to pro'duce	The farmers couldn't produce enough produce.
'conduct	to con'duct	They conducted an enquiry into the conduct of the team.
'research	to re'search	We're researching the need for more research!

Some noun/verb pairs, however, differ in form, spelling and/or pronunciation. Study and read these pairs. The noun ends in a voiceless consonant (/s/, /f/, etc.), the verb in a voiced consonant (/z/, /v/, etc.).

Noun	Verb	Noun	Verb
a'buse /s/	to a'buse /z/	(a) be'lief	to be'lieve
ad'vice	to ad'vise	(a) 'breath	to 'breathe
a 'choice	to 'choose	'cloth	to 'clothe
a de'vice	to de'vise	a 'half	to 'halve
an ex'cuse	to ex'cuse	(a) 'life	to 'live
a 'house	to 'house	'proof	to 'prove
(a) 'use	to 'use	a 'shelf	to 'shelve

2 Game: *Read that!* (see Teacher's Guide Unit 10)

3 Study this passage. Where do you think it's taken from? Be prepared to read it aloud.

> Even if there were photographic records of faith healing, many scientists would still discount the event as 'not proved' and would suspect anything that could not be subjected to scientific research. Belief in something means accepting it, with or without proof. The very subject of faith healing conflicts with a scientific approach to things, and the phenomenon itself is, it must be admitted, open to a great deal of abuse, if not trickery.

Oral Interview preparation

1 Study this photo carefully and then answer the questions.

About the photo

1 Where do you think this photo was taken? Why do you think that?
2 What do you think the man (in the centre) is doing? What has he got draped round his shoulders? And what do you think he might be holding?
3 Why are the other people keeping away from the area the man is walking/running on?

Personal

1 Do you think *you* could do what the man's doing – walk across hot coals?
2 Can you snuff out a candle between your fingers? Isn't that the same kind of thing?

General

1 Have you heard of people firewalking in other countries? If so, where?
2 Do you believe it can be done? If so, how do you think it is done? If not, why don't you think it's possible?
3 What other ways do you know (or have you read) about in which people exercise 'mind over matter'?
4 Are there any special festivals or events in your country that a visitor should see?
5 Are there any customs in your country that a foreign visitor should know about?

2 Reading aloud

Read these passages silently and then read one aloud. When
preparing to read aloud, remember these points:
a) Read it carefully right through to make sure you understand it.
b) Look carefully at the punctuation, so that you know where to pause,
   and so that you know whether a sentence is a statement, a question
   or an exclamation! Remember than an exclamation mark will
   indicate surprise, disgust, or some other emotion.
c) Look carefully at the vocabulary for any pronunciation or stress
   problems.
d) You will be asked to identify the probable context of the passage, so
   from your reading try to work out or guess who might have said
   what you have read, or where it might have appeared in print.

1 We decided to subject the whole experiment to the utmost scrutiny. In order to do this, we recorded on film the progress of the event from start to finish. Indeed, not only did we record it on film, but we had three cameras running, placed at various points around the 'performer', and we also made a sound recording. Do you know what happened the first time we tried to record it? We had a power cut just before the 'performer' began to set up his equipment! My colleagues suspected sabotage, but I was not so sure.

2 Had I not seen it myself, I would never have believed it! On the Thursday night the woman began to breathe very heavily and with extreme difficulty, and she was examined by two doctors. Although their reports regarding the cause of the woman's illness conflicted, they agreed on one thing: she had only a few hours to live. The following morning, that was Friday, I visited the house and there she was, large as life, sitting at the kitchen table enjoying a hearty breakfast. All her family would say was that they had called in a faith healer in the night . . .

3 Game: *Just a minute!* (see Teachers Guide Unit 5)

4 Role play: 'Mind over Matter'

Decide in pairs who is going to argue for a belief in mind over matter
and who against. Then individually make brief notes of the main points
you wish to use for your argument and against your partner's.

Some useful language for your discussion:
a) *Presenting*   The first thing I want to/must say is that . . .
   your argument: Secondly, . . . /Thirdly, . . . /And finally, . . .
                      While/Although/Since/As (it's difficult to . . .), nevertheless . . .
b) *Questioning:*   While I agree (with you) that . . ., what about . . .?
                      You said that . . . . Do you really mean/think that . . .?
                      Although you said that . . ., don't you think that . . .?
c) *Interrupting:*   I wonder if I might come in here.
                      I'm sorry to butt in, but . . .
                      I'd just like to say (at this point) that . . .

Now begin your discussion of 'mind over matter'.

5 Class discussion

What do you really think?

11 Television, Films and Photography

Style

In the Proficiency Paper 1 (Reading Comprehension) you may have to
answer questions that require an understanding of an author's attitude,
purpose and intended audience as revealed by his or her style and
choice of language.

Read the two passages on these pages and do exercises 1–4 (below) in
pairs. Passage A is concerned with television in general; Passage B
with TV news reporting.

1

1 Decide what the authors think of television and television reporting respectively.
2 List the vocabulary or phrases which reveal these attitudes.
3 Which of the following adjectives best describe the tone of these passages?

humorous; serious; cynical; ironical; cruel; weary; sad; angry; protesting;
resigned; objective; impartial; bright; energetic; unhappy; tense; worried

Make lists for passage A and passage B.
4 Pick out and list words or phrases that justify your opinions.
5 Compare your opinions with the rest of the class, and justify your reasons.
6 What kind of publications do you think these passages come from? Why?
7 Complete the detailed work on the two passages.

A A continuous commentary or mirror of 'real' life
had been created on television. To switch on the set
when the day's viewing started, with one's mind
slightly turned down, or in a bit of a fever, or very
5 tired, and to watch, steadily, through the hours, as
little figures, diminished people, dressed up like
cowboys or like bus drivers or like Victorians, with
this or that accent, in this or that setting, sometimes a
hospital, sometimes an office or an aircraft, some-
10 times 'real' or sometimes imaginary (that is to say,
the product of somebody's, or some team's, imagination), it was exactly like what could be seen when one
turned one's vision outwards again towards life: it
was as if an extreme of variety had created a
15 sameness, a nothingness, as if humanity had said yes
to becoming a meaningless flicker of people dressed
in varying kinds of clothes to kill each other ('real'
and 'imaginary') or play various kinds of sport, or
discuss art, love, sex, ethics (in 'plays' or in 'life'),
20 for after an hour or so, it was impossible to tell the
difference between news, plays, reality, imagination,
truth, falsehood. If someone—from a year's exile in a
place without television, let alone a visitor from
Mars— had dropped in for an evening's 'viewing,'
25 then he might well have believed that this steady
stream of little pictures, all so consistent in tone or
feel, were part of some continuous single programme
written or at least 'devised' by some boss director
who had arranged, to break monotony, slight vari-
30 ations in costume, or setting (office, park, ballet,
school, aircraft, war), and with a limited team of
actors—for the same people had to play dozens of
different roles.

It was all as bland and meaningless as steamed
35 white bread; yet composed of the extremes of nasti-
ness in a frenzy of dislocation, disconnection, as if
one stood on a street corner and watched half a dozen
variations of the human animal pass in a dozen
different styles of dress and face.

Detailed work

1 The author's style reflects the constantly changing
programmes she mentions. How?
2 Why does the author repeat the word 'turned' (ll.4
and 13)?
3 Why are 'plays' and 'life' written in inverted
commas (l.19)?
4 How does the author emphasise the idea that TV
programmes are 'part of some continuous single
programme' (l.27)?

B   Bev, shoulders straight, chest out, legs like water, reported for duty as usual at eight in the morning at Penn's Chocolate Works. There was a picket waiting for him. There were policemen, chewing their straps.
5   The police, though reluctantly, grabbed a man who threw a small stone at Bev, even though he missed.

'Whose side are you bloody rozzers on?' went the shout.

10   'You know the law as well as what I do,' said the sergeant unhappily. A van from Thames Television drew up. Bev waited. His act would have no validity unless available for the world to witness. This was the new way. It's Really Real when it's Seen on the
15   Screen. Jeff Fairclough got out, hands deep in smart raincoat, red hair waving in the breeze. A man with a hand-held camera and a recordist with a tape-recorder followed. Fairclough and Bev nodded to each other. He had telephoned Fairclough the pre-
20   vious evening. Fairclough had once been a colleague, a teacher of English until the advent of the new syllabus. ('Usage is the only law. *You was* is the form used by eighty-five per cent of the British population. *You was* is therefore correct. The pedantic may reflect
25   that this was the regular form used by pedants like Jonathan Swift in the eighteenth century.') Bev and the team marched through the open gateway. The strikers put on a great act of snarling and cursing for the camera. The sound recordist didn't record. They
30   could get the swearing from stock. Bev led the way to the executive wing. Young Mr Penn, very nervous, came forth to meet them. The man with the tape-recorder put his headphones on, switched on, gave a thumbs up to Fairclough, who said: 'Action.'

Detailed work

1   What does 'legs like water' (l.1) mean?
2   What impression is given of the police in ll.4–11?
3   What are the connotations of 'It's Really Real when it's Seen on the Screen' (ll.14–15)?
4   What are the connotations of 'red hair waving in the breeze' (l.16)?
5   Why does the author include the contents of the brackets (ll.22–26)?
6   What are the connotations of 'snarling and cursing' (l.28)? What impressions do we therefore get of the strikers?
7   What are the connotations of the word 'Action' (l.34)?

2   Connotations

According to the Penguin English Dictionary, a connotation = 'implication; associations and emotional overtones of a word: all that is implied by a word or term'. Connotations can play a very large part in conveying a writer's message.

1   Association Game (in pairs): In turns, close your eyes while your partner reads to you the words in one of the lists below. After each word, tell your partner what images or associations this word brings to mind. Then swap roles and continue with the words in the second list.

List A: London; beach; caviar; motor bike; computer
List B: opera; sports car; wine; velvet; butterflies;

2   How many of the associations did you share? Some connotations are personal and some are culturally shared. Can an author work with both kinds?

3   Words may have positive, negative or neutral connotations, for example:

POSITIVE	'little angels'	freedom-fighter
NEUTRAL	children	rebel
NEGATIVE	brats	terrorist

Discuss the connotations of the following words and label them appropriately '(pos.)', '(neg.)' or '(neu.)':

news, propaganda;   a journalist, a newsmonger;   to edit, to write, to scribble;
to stroll, to prowl, to wander;   a scent, a stench, a smell;
a bureaucrat, a technocrat, a civil servant; to educate, to enlighten, to indoctrinate

General discussion

1 What, for you, are the connotations of TV? Note them down. Compare your notes with the rest of the class. Do you seem to approve or disapprove of television?

2 Do you agree that TV makes it hard to distinguish between real life and the imaginary? If so, what could be the consequences of this? Do you see these consquences anywhere in today's society?

3 Should the contents of TV programmes and films (also in the cinema) be censored at all, especially with regard to sex, violence or politics? Or should every individual have the option of making his own choice about whether to watch something or not?

Discussion on a text

Read this passage and then discuss the questions.

The use of the word 'imitation' reminds me that I ought to make some more comments on the risk of people imitating what they see on the screen in the way of crime or violence. First there was always a risk of children acting out scenes which could be dangerous. For example I remember a woman who was head of an infants school telling me that she had happened to look out of her window when the children were in the playground and had seen them putting a small boy on a chair with a noose round his neck and the rope over the branch of a tree; fortunately she was in time to intervene before the child was hanged. I remember a film of no particular merit in which the hero who was imprisoned had escaped by electrocuting his guard, the technique of doing this being shown in detail. This was the kind of scene which we would cut for these reasons.

In films for young people and adults we always tried to keep off the screen any details of criminal techniques, such as how to open a locked door with a piece of celluloid, or how to open a safe; if we were consulted before production I used to advise that the details should not be shown. When I gave talks in prisons about film censorship I invariably had full support for this, since fathers who were in prison for criminal offences did not want their children to embark on crime.

Every time I gave a talk in a prison someone used to mention the French film *Rififi* made by Jules Dassin in 1954. This remarkable film showed in great detail a robbery of a jeweller's shop, the robbery sequence lasting about half an hour and being backed only by natural sound – one of the most brilliant film sequences of all time. I remember our discussions at the time. We took into account the fact that the robbery was accomplished only with the use of elaborate and obviously expensive equipment, and that only the most experienced and skilled criminals could possibly imitate it; we believed therefore that it was relatively safe. When talking in prisons some years later I learned that there had been several robberies in which the techniques had been copied, so perhaps we were wrong.

'A scene from Rififi'

1 What do you think is or was the job or profession of the person who wrote this passage?

2 Do you approve or disapprove of the two censorship decisions mentioned in the passage? Why?

3 How would you describe the style and tone of this passage? Does it make use of connotation? If so, where and why? If not, why not, do you think?

4 What kind of publication do you think this passage comes from? Give reasons.

Vocabulary

1 Would you like to be a professional photographer? Discuss why, or why not.

2 Read the passage below quite quickly and answer this one question: Does the woman photographer in the passage seem to have enjoyed her career?

3 Now do these exercises.

1 *Guessing the meaning of words from context:* Find the following words or phrases in the passage and work out from the context what they must mean. Write down your deductions and compare them with those of others in the class.

cliquey	lift a finger
posturers	snapshot
patronage	posterity
dreary	crooked
courted	fraud

Were there any you could *not* work out from the context? Why?

2 *Connotations:* What are the connotations of the following words from the passage?

a pathfinder	paperwork
cheap	tea-drinking
posturer	

3 *Vocabulary areas:* Go through the passage to pick out and list all the words or phrases connected with photography. What other words do you know from this area? Add them to your list, then compare with other students.

NOTE: Some of the photography vocabulary in the passage is used with a double meaning to refer both to photography and to Maude Coffin Pratt. Which are used like this and why?

4 *Collocations:* Generally speaking, what can be *promoted*?
What or who is *courted*?
What can receive *exposure*?
What can you have *vintages of*?
What or who can be *crooked*?

My pictures, the same pictures, appeared everywhere. The show traveled, the photographs were reproduced in magazines, my early work was rediscovered and promoted. I was seen to have been an important Twenties pathfinder, one of the few American photographers who had not
5   gone to Europe. (I hadn't thought to do so, but I would not have gone for anything, since Europe – the cheap franc, the cliquey artists, the crowd-pleasers and posturers – represented to me the most hideous kind of patr...iage.) Blacks were in fashion and of course I'd done them by the bushel basket. At the dreariest time of my life I'd done my funniest and most
10 hopeful pictures; at my most hopeful I had done desperately tormented shots. When I had sought work I had been ignored, and when I was no longer looking for it I was courted. Now my fame was consolidated. I must have seemed to many people incredibly busy with all this exposure. I wasn't. Papa did all the paperwork. I didn't lift a finger.
15   And, as often happens, my fame became an aspect of others' – the general public confused me with other woman photographers of my own vintage: Margaret Bourke-White, Imogen Cunningham, Ann Brigman, Berenice Abbot, Dorothea Lange, and even older ones like Gertrude Käsebier.
20   I was too detached to be offended. I regarded this woman, Maude Coffin Pratt, with a mixture of awe, scepticism and amusement. What an engine of creation she was! What depth of field! What a glad eye! I could never live up to her achievement (her pictures *were* rather good), so I didn't try. I still got many requests to do pictures – it was an effect of the war in Europe, the
25 urgency that the present must be caught on film, a kind of souvenir-hunting, since the world would change out of recognition. It was the superstitious deception of the photograph as a historical record, the snapshot for posterity, as a photograph of the Chinese wedding is as much a part of the ceremony as the tea-drinking. Or the other sort of picture, the
30 view-camera taxidermy of buildings soon to be bombed, the portraits of crooked political bosses who expect to be voted out of office or jailed for fraud.

Exam guidance

Complete the test on this page before reading the opposite page.

SECTION A (Time: 8 minutes)

In this section you must choose the word or phrase which best completes each sentence. For each question, 1 to 10, indicate on your answer sheet the letter A, B, C or D against the number of the question.

1 The dog _____ at its chain in irritation.
   A snapped B snarled C whined D ate

2 Everyone congratulated the TV service on its excellent documentary _____.
   A serials B series C sequels D soap operas

3 His _____ manner made many people suspicious of him.
   A grey B blank C mild D colourless

4 All the participants solemnly _____ on the Bible to keep the secret.
   A cursed B swore C vowed D promised

5 A _____ of interest briefly crossed his face at the mention of her name.
   A flicker B trace C gleam D hint

6 The extremely _____ weather was beginning to get on everyone's nerves.
   A bland B dreary C dim D gluey

7 Not once did I see him _____ a finger to help in the home.
   A twiddle B shift C move D lift

8 In some countries the cinema industry receives a _____ from the State.
   A donation B mortgage C credit D subsidy

9 _____ it not been for the intolerable heat, we would have gone out.
   A But B If C Had D Should

10 The protestors carried _____ and wore badges to publicise their cause.
    A banners B hoardings C pamphlets D advertisements

EXAM ADVICE: Ten golden rules for Reading Comprehension: Section A

1 Watch your *timing*. Don't spend more than 20 minutes on the 25 questions in this Section.

2 Read the *instructions* very carefully.

3 Make sure you put *the right letter* on your answer sheet.

4 Make sure you write your answer against the *right question number* on the answer sheet.

5 *Don't get stuck on one question*. If you can't do it, leave it, go on and come back to it at the end.

ANSWERS   EXPLANATIONS OF ANSWERS

1A	One clue to the answer is the word *irritation*, as *snarling* implies anger and *whining* implies helplessness and even pain. A dog will often *snap at* something when it is irritated. Another clue is in the grammar: you can't '*eat at*' something.
2B	One clue to the answer is the word *documentary* which collocates with *a series* (= a number of programmes without a story line). *Serials* and *soap operas* are both fictional programmes with a story line. *Sequels* are follow-ups to books, films or programmes. You would need some reference therefore to a previous or initial programme for the sentence to make sense for C.
3C	The answer relies on collocation. You can't speak of '*a grey, blank* or *colourless manner*' but a person can have *a mild manner*.
4B	The answer relies again on collocation, this time *to swear on the Bible* (where *swear*= take an oath). *To curse* means to use bad language. You can say he *vowed/promised to keep the secret*, but neither of these collocates with the phrase *on the Bible*.
5A	One clue to the answer lies in the phrase *crossed his face* because it implies movement. Besides which, we talk about *a flicker of interest*, but *a hint (or a ghost) of a smile*. We also talk of *a trace of interest* (often in *no trace of interest*), but it would not be used with the verb *crossed* as in this sentence.
6B	Partly a question of collocation again: *weather* can be *dreary* (but not *bland* or *gluey* or *dim*).
7D	Collocation again: we say *not raise* or *not lift a finger* (= not do anything). *Shift* simply means *to move*. What does *to twiddle your fingers* mean?
8D	*A donation*= a gift, especially for a good cause, *A mortgage*= money lent for buying a house which is repaid in instalments. *Credit*= a system shops offer to enable customers to 'buy now and pay later'. *A subsidy*= money paid by a government or official body to a firm or organisation to help or support it.
9C	A pure structural item. For the other choices to work, the sentences would have to be: *But for the intolerable heat, . . .* and *If it had not been for the intolerable heat, . . .*, and *Should* cannot be used at the beginning of a sentence with a Past Conditional.
10A	*Hoardings*= high fences or boards on which advertisements are stuck. You wouldn't *carry* pamphlets to publicise a cause; you would hand them out or distribute them. And you wouldn't *carry* advertisements, either.

6 Don't leave any question *unanswered*. Always write something.

7 *Read the whole sentence* before answering.

8 Consider the *meaning of the whole sentence*.

9 Look also for *grammatical collocational* and *connotational* clues to the answer.

10 Well before the exam, *read as much and as widely* in English as possible.

Complete the test on this page before reading the opposite page.

SECTION B   (Time: 13 minutes)

In this section you will find after the passage a number of questions or unfinished statements about the passage, each with four suggested answers or ways of finishing. You must choose the one which you think fits best. For each question, 11 to 15, indicate on your answer sheet the letter A, B, C or D against the number of the question.

'Impossible,' said the friendly lady, 'films today are impossible. I simply can't understand them.' You might, I said, try the film on locally, I think you might like it. And indeed this film is easy to understand: none of the sudden cuts, the unexplained shifts in time and place, the secret movements of character common in the contemporary movie. One hesitates to call it old-
5 fashioned, for the phrase can be deterrent and one doesn't want to harm this beautifully acted film. But the piece isn't designed to please the under twenty-fives who make up the current audience. It is about elderly people – elderly people in their relations with a younger generation, but basically people who feel the passing of time and by now haven't got ahead of them the decades which younger characters take for granted.
10 It is the story of an annual visit to a house and a lake in the quiet of New England woods. The Thayers come here every year; he is eighty and feels it, she is in her late sixties and resilient. Their daughter joins them; she doesn't get on with her father, she suspects he wanted a boy. This year she brings a new lover whom she will presently marry, and with him his thirteen-year-old son. When the younger pair go off on holiday they leave the boy with the ageing couple. The centre of the tale
15 becomes the relationship between the old man, unwelcoming, crotchety, a born deliverer of the caustic rebuff, and the child of the city whose recreation is the pursuit of what he calls 'chicks' and whose whole conversation is punctuated by swear words.
    The film then reveals its essential theme, reconciliation. Everybody is reconciled, the generations smoothe out their differences and learn to love everybody. And yes, the general goodwill belongs to
20 another age of the cinema; it is satisfying, it isn't over-cosy, but today it is a bit much. Or it would be if it weren't for the acting.

11 The person who mentioned the film on locally

  A was friendly.
  B recommended it.
  C was puzzled by many of today's films.
  D suggested her friend should see it.

12 The author of the passage thinks the film

  A is hopelessly old-fashioned.
  B is hopelessly old-fashioned but well acted.
  C employs many simple techniques.
  D is right for someone of her age.

13 What is the film about?

  A Reconciliation between generations.
  B Family relationships.
  C People growing old.
  D A holiday in the country.

14 The author of the passage thinks that the film

  A will be generally well liked.
  B will only appeal to old people.
  C will not be well received.
  D will have only limited appeal.

15 This passage was written

  A in order to promote the film.
  B as a review of the film.
  C to describe the film for a film catalogue.
  D to recommend the film to a friendly lady.

ANSWERS   EXPLANATIONS OF ANSWERS

11B	The lines to look at are ll.1–2 and then work out who said what. The words of the friendly lady are in inverted commas whereas the other person's are not.
12C	The lines to look at are ll.2–9, plus the rest of the passage. Firstly, the author shows in ll.4–5 a certain fondness for certain old-fashioned things, so A and B cannot be right. Secondly, nowhere in the passage does the author give us any indication of her age; therefore, D is impossible. And thirdly, you need to understand the function of the colon (:) in l.3. The words on either side of a colon always refer to each other, therefore 'none of the sudden cuts . . . movie' must qualify 'this film is easy to understand'.
13A	The lines to look at are ll.6–17. Firstly, you might be tempted by ll.6–9 to think that C is the right answer, but by reading carefully you will realise that nowhere does the passage say that the film is about growing old: about people feeling time passing by . . . yes; about elderly people relating to younger people . . . yes; but growing old . . . no. Secondly, you might be tempted by ll.10–14 to think that the film is about B or D, but read on . . . ll.14–17 tell us it isn't and that the family relationships and the holiday in the country are just settings for the story. The answer is given in l.18, reinforcing what was suggested in the previous lines.
14D	The lines to look at are ll.1–6 and ll.19–21. This answer also requires careful reading. Nowhere does the passage say either A or C, so we are left with B or D. In l.6 the author says the film won't please the under–25s, but in ll.2–3 she recommends the film – not to younger people, as we have just seen, but to the over-25s, who are not generally considered 'old'. And finally, the whole tone of the piece implies that the film will not be a raving success, but will have limited appeal.
15B	A is obviously wrong because the passage not only contains negative criticism, but is also too detailed for promotional literature. C must also be wrong because descriptions in film catalogues must be short and factual. Neither is there anything in the passage to indicate that D is correct. The answer therefore must be B, as can also be seen from the content of the passage as a whole.

EXAM ADVICE: Reading Comprehension: Section B

1   Points 1–6 of the Section A EXAM ADVICE all apply here, except that in Section B you have to answer 15 multiple-choice questions on three or more texts in about 40 minutes. Do *not* spend all your time on the first passage, then have to rush the others. Divide your time out proportionally, and be strict with yourself.

2   Read the multiple-choice questions, and then the passage and the questions again, *before* answering them.

3   Locate the right part(s) of the text when doing each question. The answer may span a few or many lines and be found in one or various parts of the text.

4   Read ALL FOUR possible answers for each question and don't choose the first one you read which *happens* to look right. It may be right, but it may not. Check against the other possible answers and the text. And read all possible answers *in detail*!

5   Don't expect the next answer to come in the lines of the text following the last answer. It may or may not.

6   Don't think that because a word appears in the text and in an answer, this answer must therefore be right. Read round the word in both to see how it is qualified or referred to in the same, previous or following sentence(s).

7   Watch out for the meaning of punctuation and conjunctions, and what words like *it, he, she, too, so*, etc. refer to. These words can be very important

12 People, Places, Experiences, Events

PAPER 2: COMPOSITION

1 In small groups, describe the following to one another:

1 Last weekend
2 Last year's holidays
3 Your first day at school

4 A teacher you had at school
who stands out in your mind

2 Individually, think about what you and your colleagues have just told each other and about other descriptions of people, places, actions, experiences and events that you've read or heard recently. Then note down what in your opinion makes a story or a description interesting and worth paying attention to.

3 In the Proficiency Paper 2 (Composition) there is often a descriptive or narrative composition title. Here are some examples of titles of this kind. Which are descriptive and which are narrative?

1 'A holiday with a difference.' Describe this holiday.
2 An official ceremony I once attended.
3 The most exciting thing that has ever happened to me.

4 My hero/heroine.
5 Life on an ideal 'Planet Earth'.
6 'The night the burglars got in.' Describe what happened that night.

Note the kinds of things we usually describe or narrate:

(un)typical
(un)pleasant
(least) favourite
unusual/different
imaginary
} {
influences
feelings/emotions/reactions
experiences/events/actions
people
places

4 Discussion

Read this extract from a newspaper article and discuss the questions.

IT IS a wasteland of grey Victorian buildings where slumbering figures occupy all the doorways, hallways and flat roofs. It is the Bowery, New York's Skid Row on the Lower East side, the world famous reservation of bums and alcoholics and drug addicts.

You can still see the old be-whiskered men clasping empty liquor bottles like lovers or the young men with parchment skins and hollow eyes wasting away on doorsteps, but among them now is a new Bowery breed reared by the recession – jobless, homeless, drifting teenage youths, who are competing with the winos and the junkies for beds in the Bowery's shelter for the homeless and for the still vacant doorways.

It is a shock at first to see the newcomers because they appear so full of life compared with the Bowery's more familiar inhabitants. But talking to them changes that impression and then they don't seem nearly so out-of-place. Mentally, they display a strange passivity that matches the state of mind of the winos and the junkies, a freezing of the will as if they have given up hope of improving their condition and so have settled here at the official bottom, the notorious end of the road, among their peers.

1 Why did the author of this article choose to describe this particular scene?
2 What emotion does he feel towards the people he describes?
3 Is this description boring? interesting? useful? tedious? superfluous? commonplace? hackneyed? Why?
4 Would you choose to describe this scene, or one like it? If so, who for? If not, why not?

84

Analysing a description

1 Read this passage and discuss the questions.

My first image of my Mother was of a beautiful woman, strong, bounteous, but with a gravity of breeding that was always visible beneath her nervous chatter. She became, in a few years, both bent and worn, her healthy opulence quickly gnawed away by her later trials and hungers. It is in this second stage that I remembered her best, for in this stage she remained the longest. I can see her prowling about the kitchen, dipping a rusk into a cup of tea, with hair loose-tangled, and shedding pins, clothes shapelessly humped around her, eyes peering sharply at some revelation of the light, crying Ah or Oh or There, or reciting Tennyson and demanding my understanding.

With her love of finery, her unmade beds, her litters of unfinished scrapbooks, her taboos, superstitions, and prudishness, her remarkable dignity, her pity for the persecuted, her awe of the gentry, and her detailed knowledge of the family trees of all the Royal Houses of Europe, she was a disorganized mass of unreconciled denials, a servant girl born to silk. Yet in spite of all this, she fed our oafish wits with steady, imperceptible shocks of beauty. Though she tortured our patience and exhausted our nerves, she was, all the time, building up around us, by the unconscious revelations of her loves, an interpretation of man and the natural world so unpretentious and easy that we never recognized it then, yet so true that we never forgot it.

Nothing now that I ever see that has the edge of gold around it – the change of a season, a jewelled bird in a bush, the eyes of orchids, water in the evening, a thistle, a picture, a poem – but my pleasure pays some brief duty to her. She tried me at times to the top of my bent. But I absorbed from birth, as now I know, the whole earth through her jaunty spirit.

1 What impression does it leave you with? Did you like it or not?
   Is it a good description, do you think? Why?/Why not?
2 Why are there three paragraphs in this description? What is each
   about?

2 Read the passage again and note down on a piece of paper which of
the following features you think are present in the passage and which
are not.

1 A use of contrast
2 A climax
3 Variety of sentence length
4 Precise descriptive vocabulary
5 Personal revelations

6 A switch from narrative to dialogue
7 A striking opening sentence
8 A conclusion
9 Quickly moving sentences
10 Images

Compare your lists with a partner. Why are certain features absent from
or present in the passage?

3 Guided Composition Work: Describe a) a good friend, and b) a relation.

1 Make notes for each as follows: Paragraph 1 – Physical description
                                  Paragraph 2 – Description of character
                                  Paragraph 3 – Description of the influence
                                                 this person has had on you

2 Describe these people orally to someone else in the class.

3 Write the descriptions for homework, incorporating as many of the
   features in **2** above as are appropriate.

Choosing appropriate vocabulary

1 Imagine the following situation:

A woman in a library reads some bad news. Her reaction is to feel sick and ill. She gets up and goes outside, but feeling too ill to drive her own car, she calls for a taxi. The taxi-driver notices she's not well, so he helps her into the taxi.

2 In pairs,

1 list suitable vocabulary and phrases to describe how the woman looked, sounded, moved and reacted at each stage in the story:

2 list any time words (adverbs, conjunctions or phrases) that you think could be useful when telling the story; and

3 write the story as vividly as you can.

3 Now read this version and compare your story with it.

She sat down and read. Her mouth went dry. Suddenly it was if her consciousness was being gripped by a huge, invisible force and loosened from its moorings. The page seemed to recede in front of her, and she found herself reading it down a long misty tunnel.

For a moment she thought she was going to faint. Her face felt white and tight, the colour seemed to have drained out of everything around her. And she was afraid she might be sick. In a whirl of light-headedness she got up, descended the stairs and came out into the bloodless daylight. As soon as she saw her car she knew she was unable to drive it. Still afraid her legs might give way under her she walked the few yards to Kensington High Street and signalled the first of the taxis that stood in the rank to her right.

When the driver saw her face, and she gave him in a croaking voice an address only a few hundred yards away, he said with genuine concern: 'You feeling ill lady?' She nodded dumbly, and he leapt out of the cab and came round to help her in.

4 Detailed work on the passage

1 Pick out the words and phrases in the passage which are particularly exact and descriptive. Compare them with words and phrases you used in exercise **2**.

2 Why are there three paragraphs in the passage? What is each about?

3 Pick out all the time words used in the passage. What other words could they be replaced by? What changes in sentence construction would they require?

NOTE: Narratives typically contain a variety of different time words. Here are some more of them:
immediately; finally; gradually; while; eventually; for a while.
What synonyms do you know for each of these words or phrases?

Structuring a description

1 On the right is an extract from a diary (George Orwell's). It is written in an interesting style – part note form, part connected prose.
Read the extract and work out:

.1 what topic progression it follows.

2 where you would make paragraphs to turn it into a full prose passage.

3 what items or lines would have to be changed to form connected prose, and how.

4 which words and phrases are particularly exact and descriptive.

2 Discuss and describe

'One of the most appalling places I have ever seen.'

1 Have you ever been to a place that appalled you? Why did it? What made it so especially awful?

2 Note down some aspects of the place that deserve description.

3 Arrange these aspects into a logical order for an overall description.

4 Using your notes, describe the place as vividly as possible to someone else in the class.

5 Write a short description of the place, then exchange descriptions with others in the class. Read and discuss them.

Had a very long and exhausting day (I am now continuing this March 4th) being shown every quarter of Sheffield on foot and by tram. I have now traversed almost the whole city. It seems to me, by daylight, one of the most appalling places I have ever seen. In
5 whichever direction you look you see the same landscape of monstrous chimneys pouring forth smoke which is sometimes black and sometimes of a rosy tint said to be due to sulphur. You can smell the sulphur in the air all the while. All buildings are blackened within a year or two of being put up. Halting at one place
10 I counted the factory chimneys I could see and there were 33. But it was very misty as well as smoky – there would have been many more visible on a clear day. I doubt whether there are any architecturally decent buildings in the town. The town is very hilly (said to be built on seven hills, like Rome) and everywhere streets of mean little
15 houses blackened by smoke run up at sharp angles, paved with cobbles which are purposely set unevenly to give horses etc. a grip. At night the hilliness creates fine effects because you look across from one hillside to the other and see the lamps twinkling like stars. Huge jets of flame shoot periodically out of the roofs of the
20 foundries (many working night shifts at present) and show a splendid rosy colour through the smoke and steam. When you get a glimpse inside you see enormous fiery serpents of red-hot and white-hot (really lemon-coloured) iron being rolled out into rails. In the central slummy part of the town are the small workshops of the
25 'little bosses', i.e. smaller employers who are making chiefly cutlery. I don't think I ever in my life saw so many broken windows. Some of these workshops have hardly a pane of glass in their windows and you would not believe they were inhabitable if you did not see the employees, mostly girls, at work inside.

Descriptive and narrative composition writing

The ingredients

Pages 84–87 show us that well-written descriptions and narrations depend on:

1 *Having something to say* that is somehow different from the ordinary, the usual and the expected. This is what captures the reader's attention.

2 *Good planning* that gives progression, direction and purpose to what is written.

3 *Good paragraphing* that highlights new aspects of the general theme of the piece of writing and reveals the order chosen at the planning stage.

4 *Well chosen vocabulary, phrases and imagery* that pinpoint and enrich exact and important detail.

5 *Varying sentence length* that captures mood, atmosphere and the rhythm of action or observation and arrests and holds the reader's attention.

Homework exercise   (Recommended time: 1 hour)

Write the plan and the composition for one of the titles on page 84 (exercise **3**).

Exam guidance

Below is an example of the sort of Composition Paper you can expect in the Proficiency exam. Read the Paper carefully and then answer these questions:

1 How many compositions must you write?
2 How long is the exam?
3 How much time would you spend on each of the following:
   a) reading the whole Paper?
   b) writing the plan for your first composition?
   c) writing your first composition?
   d) checking your first composition?
   e) writing the plan for your second composition?
   f) writing your second composition?
   g) checking your second composition?
4 Would you have time to write a rough *and* a fair copy of each composition?
5 Which composition titles would you choose? Those that a) interest you most? b) seem linguistically easiest? or c) a combination of a) and b)? Why?

PAPER 2 **COMPOSITION** (Time: 2 hours)

Write two only of the following composition exercises. Your answers must follow exactly the instructions given. Write in pen, not pencil. You are allowed to make alterations, but see that your work is clear and easy to read.

1 'The first day in my first job.' Write a descriptive account. (About 350 words)

2 'The rich get rich while the poor get poorer.' Is this an accurate description of today's society? Discuss in about 350 words.

3 As Public Relations Officer of a national airline you have just received an irate letter from a customer complaining about the quality of your company's service, its standards of hygiene, its safety precautions and prices. Write a placating letter of reply to this customer. (About 200 words)

4 The historical figure I most admire, and why. (About 200 words)

5 (This will be a choice of questions on the prescribed texts.)

EXAM ADVICE: Composition

1 Read the whole paper before choosing titles.

2 Read and obey the instructions.

3 Make all compositions *100%* relevant to the titles.

4 Make your compositions of the right length.

5 Don't spend all your time on the 1st composition and neglect the 2nd.

Revision of composition writing

1 Planning

> 1 'The first day in my first job.' Write a descriptive account. (About 350 words)

Below is a series of notes on what possibly to include in this composition written in random order. Read through them and then
1 decide if they are all relevant to the title; and
2 put them in logical order as a plan, indicating what would go in which paragraph.

> How I got the job – What the place looked like – What I wore – How I felt – What the boss was like – My age – How much I got paid – What the job was – What the other people were like – How I felt at the end of the day – My situation (why I was there) – Why I wanted the job – What happened during the day – What the job involved – How long I stayed in the job.

NOTE: You could do this composition even if you had never worked!

2 Planning, paragraphing, opening paragraphs and useful vocabulary

> 2 'The rich get rich and the poor get poorer.' Is this an accurate description of today's society? Discuss in about 350 words.

1 Discuss the topic as a class.
2 In groups, draw up two lists, one with examples supporting the statement in the title, and one with examples to disprove it. What conclusion can you draw from the two lists in relation to the statement in the title?
3 Individually write a plan for the above composition title in 10–15 minutes. Think in terms of 1st paragraph, 2nd paragraph, 3rd paragraph.
4 Examine and criticise one another's plans, paying particular attention to: amount of content, relevance and ordering.
5 Which of the following would provide the best introduction to this composition? Why?
   a) This quotation is perfectly true and I think this situation is absolutely disgusting. We should try and change it by . . .
   b) Although this statement may well be true, there is little we can do about the situation it describes, since . . .
   c) If we look around at today's world, we can see examples that both prove and disprove this statement.
   d) In this composition I will first look at some examples which seem to suggest that this quotation is correct, then at others which seem to disprove it, and then I will draw my conclusions.
   e) It's hard to know what's going on in the world today as the media present us with such a one-sided view of things, but my reading and my own eyes suggest to me that it could well be true. Let's see why . . .
6 Remember the following vocabulary which is very useful in composition writing:
firstly; in my opinion; in short; as regards; . . .; despite; besides; however; e.g.; that is to say; lastly.
What synonyms do you know for each of these words or phrases?

3 Style, planning, degree of formality, joining words

3 As Public Relations Officer of a national airline you have just received an irate letter from a customer complaining about the quality of your company's service, its standards of hygiene, its safety precautions and prices. Write a placating letter of reply to this customer. (About 200 words)

1 Complete the blanks in the following letter with appropriate words or phrases:

Dear ....,
.... for your letter of 3rd September. First ......,
I .... like to say .... very surprised I was to receive your
letter. Our company rarely receives complaints and it was .... most
disturbing for us to receive .... a letter.
  I would like to .... with your points one ...... one; ....,
.... what you said about the quality of our service,
...... I say that our company has always done its .... to ensure its
customers' excellent service. However, you may ....
.... and this I very much regret.
  Secondly, ...
....
....
....
  Thirdly, ...
....
....
....
.... , as far .... our prices ....
I'm afraid we have no control over these as they are fixed by international
agreement.
  To compensate you for the .... you may have experienced we
would be very happy to ....
Please ....
  We look ....

   Yours sincerely,

   ....
   Public Relations Officer

---

2 What do you think the plan for this letter looked like?
 Write it out paragraph by paragraph.
3 What style is the above letter written in? Note down the parts of the
 letter which reveal the style.
4 What are the words used to introduce the third, fourth and fifth
 paragraphs? What other words could be used in their place?
5 What are the different formulae employed in English to begin and end
 formal and informal letters?

4 Checking your composition

> 4 The historical figure I most admire, and why. (About 200 words)

In the heat of writing a composition it's easy to make a range of different kinds of mistakes, even though the composition might have been well planned and well timed. It is therefore *extremely important* to check your composition very carefully after you have written it, and also to make sure you leave yourself enough time for this checking.

1 The following is the first 6 lines of an introductory paragraph for the above composition title. It contains a number of mistakes, all of which have been underlined. Read through the paragraph and classify the mistakes (using the key below) by putting the appropriate letter (or letters) above each mistake. NOTE: A sentence may contain more than one kind of mistake.

   KEY: G = Grammar   V = Vocabulary   S = Spelling

   P = Punctuation   O = Organisation   ST = Style

> The historical figure I most admire is someone who has lived in my country many years ago, a long time before I born, in fact he died in May 27th, 1742. Despite he died so long ago he remains one of our most big political influences, and his wise thoughts and actions provided invaluable giudance to our polititians across the centuries. I'm going to tell you his name, it's

2 Rewrite the above paragraph correctly.
3 Organisational mistakes can be largely avoided through careful composition planning, stylistic mistakes by careful reading of the title and the use of appropriate language while writing. But punctuation, grammatical and vocabulary mistakes can be corrected mainly at the checking stage.
   English has some particularly tricky grammatical areas which often cause problems for learners of the language. Among these are:

   | Word order | | Mass nouns | | The use of *the* |

   | Tenses, especially perfect v past tenses | | Prepositions of time and place |

   | Conditional sentences |

   Which of these do you find particularly difficult? Are there any other mistakes that you know you make regularly – grammatical or other?
4 What are the two main parts of the composition title above? What would you include in each paragraph? Write a plan for the composition in 10–15 minutes.
5 Write the second paragraph of this composition (i.e. *not* the introductory paragraph), then check it very carefully looking out for the different kinds of mistakes.
6 Then exchange paragraphs with someone else in the class and check, correct and discuss each other's work.

13 Preservation and Conservation

1 Read these two definitions:

preservation	the act or action of preserving (e.g. saving a building) from destruction, or keeping a rare animal or plant in existence
conservation	the controlled use of a limited supply of natural things, to prevent waste or loss

Why are these words heard so frequently today? Can you give examples of things that need to be preserved or conserved? Why?

2 Jigsaw reading

Now, in small groups, read and study **one** of the following extracts – a, b or c – and make notes on its main points in order to report to the rest of the class what it's about. Then turn to page 94.

a)

A zoological garden can offer facilities that no other similar institution can emulate. At its best, it should be a complex laboratory, educational establishment and conservation unit. Our biological knowledge of even some of the commonest animals is embarrassingly slight and it is here that zoos can be of inestimable value in amassing information. That this can only help the ultimate conservation of an animal in the wild state is obvious, for you cannot begin to talk about conservation of a species unless you have some knowledge of how it functions. A well-run zoological garden should provide you with the facilities for just such work.

While it is obviously more desirable to study animals in the wild state, there are many aspects of animal biology which can be more easily studied in zoos and, indeed there are certain aspects that can only be studied conveniently when the animal is in a controlled environment, such as a zoo. Therefore zoological gardens – properly run zoological gardens – are enormous reservoirs of valuable data, if the animals in them are studied properly and the results recorded accurately.

Educationally, too, zoos have a most important role to play. Now that we have invented the megalopolis, we are spawning a new generation, reared without benefit of dog, cat, goldfish or budgerigar, in the upright coffins of the high-rise flats; a generation that will believe that milk comes from a bottle, without benefit of grass or cow or the intricate process between the two. This generation or its future offspring might have only the zoo to show them that creatures, other than their own kind, are trying to inhabit the earth as well.

Finally, zoos can be of immense importance in the field of conservation. Firstly, they should endeavour to breed as many of the animals in their care as possible, thus lessening the drain upon wild stocks. More important still, they can build up viable breeding groups of those species whose numbers in the wild state have dropped to an alarmingly low level. Many zoos have done, and are doing this successfully.

A bare-faced ibis reared at the Jersey Wildlife Preservation Trust

b)

'The Acropolis is in danger... After resisting the onslaughts of weather and human assailants for 2,400 years, this magnificent monument is threatened with destruction as a result of the damage which industrial civilisation has increasingly inflicted on it for a number of years past.' In these terms Mr Amadou-Mahtar M'Bow, Director-General of Unesco, launched an appeal in January 1977 to save the monuments of the Acropolis, which belong not only to Greece but to mankind as a whole.

Mr M'Bow said that today, however, the dilapidation had reached such proportions that the temples and sculptures could no longer be preserved unless a vast and complex programme of conservation work was put in hand without delay. From the technical and scientific point of view, that called for detailed studies for which it would be difficult for the Greek Government to accept sole responsibility. 'This is why' – added the Director-General of Unesco – 'I am launching here a solemn appeal to the conscience of the world so that the Acropolis may be saved.'

What is the situation today? The chemical substances now saturating the air in Athens, which over the past twenty years have perhaps done more harm to the monuments than storms and human action over the past twenty-four centuries, are making the damage even worse. The caryatids on the Erechtheion have been covered with plaster and plastic for several months and should be replaced by copies. When reproductions have taken their place, the sculptures of the Acropolis should in fact be put in safe keeping in a new museum nearby, which has however still to be built.

The frieze depicting King Cecrops on the west pediment of the Parthenon is causing concern in connection with this transfer: it is a work of high symbolic value because, as is known, Cecrops was the founder of the city. New bars of rust-proof metal (titanium has been chosen) are to replace the somewhat rudimentary ones in iron, inserted into the monuments a century ago with the laudable intention of keeping the crumbling parts together. In fact, however, the iron caused corrosion in depth, attacking the molecular structure of the marble, thereby increasing the danger of crumbling.

c)

Air pollution may at this moment be going through a trough. Its health effects are less dramatic than they were a hundred years ago, when there was more dirt and soot in the air and fog swirled through the winter streets of industrial cities.

But our relative improvement may not last, and this for two reasons, both of them concerned with the central fact in the consumption patterns of modern man – the fact of combustion. A very large part of his leaping demand for more energy is satisfied through the burning of fossil fuels, above all coal. A very large part of his personal mobility and entertainment is tied up with the internal combustion engine. In fact, we must almost think of him as a new species of centaur – half man, half automobile – and it is the heavy breathing of his motorised half that pollutes the air, invades the lungs and builds up the smog in cities.

There are, of course, other forms of pollutants from the industrial sector. The chemical industry has vastly increased the variety and exotic nature of airborne effluents. Toxic substances like mercury or asbestos or lead, which used in the main to poison only those working in particular industries, are now spread more widely in the atmosphere by a much greater variety of uses and technologies. There are also a whole range of air pollutants in agriculture. But the main source of industrial air pollution is combustion, and the two chief causes are the generation of electricity and the motor car.

Electricity generation is, however, expected to treble by 1990. Coal will still be providing at least half of this vastly increased flow. Yet, even today, half the sulphur dioxide comes from electricity plants fired with fossil fuels, 50 per cent of the oxides of nitrogen, 25 per cent of the particulates – fly ash and soot, even a measure of radioactivity. If America had to endure a tripling of these effluents over the next few decades with unchanged technologies, air pollution would clearly become unacceptably worse.

These are the risks.

Discussion

1 Each group should choose a spokesperson to report to the other
groups what their extract was about. While the reports are being given,
take notes and ask for further information or clarification as necessary
in preparation for summary writing.

2 Discuss the following:

What do you think should be done to preserve
1 cultural traditions? 2 the countryside? 3 the natural resources in the world?

In your discussions of **each** of the above, answer these questions:

What reasons are normally given for preserving /cultural traditions/? Do you agree with
them? Why?/Why not?
Can you suggest other reasons why we should preserve /cultural traditions/?
How should we go about it? Should stronger laws be made?

3 Homework exercise
Write a summary on the advantages of zoos, working from the notes
you took in **1** above only.

Use of English: Blank-filling

One part (usually test exercise 3) of Section A in the Proficiency Paper 3
(Use of English) requires you to complete blanks with a suitable word or
phrase. Like other test exercises in Section A, this is in effect a test of
grammar. In order to complete what is needed, however, you must
employ the reading skills practised in other Units in this book, and read
every word in the item, since it will contain all the clues you need.

1 There are two types of item. The first is the single sentence with a blank.
Study this example:

① ③ ④② ⑤ ②
Not only ...., but he didn't know her second name, either.

1 Remember that 'Not only . . .' is followed by an inversion construction
when it begins a sentence e.g.
Not only was I wet and lonely, but I was lost, too.
Not only did she bring her friends, but she brought all her family, too.
2 Since the second half of the sentence is negative with 'not . . . either',
the verb in the first half will almost certainly be negative, too.
3 The subject in the second half is 'he', so the subject in the first half will
almost certainly be 'he'.
4 The tense in the second half is the Simple Past, so the tense in the
first half will almost certainly be the Simple Past.
5 In the second half, 'her second name' gives a clue or pointer to 'her
first name' needed in the first half.

Such reasoning therefore suggests that the first half of the sentence should read:
'Not only did he not know her first name, . . .'
or perhaps, by the same kind of reasoning:
'Not only could he not remember her first name, . . .'

Now use the same kind of reasoning to fill in the blanks in these
sentences with a suitable word or phrase. Remember that the
completions must be correct in terms of grammar and vocabulary.

1 I would like to say how .... to receive
   your letter.
2 In spite .... 80 years old, he was still
   remarkably active.
3 Hungry ...., she had to wait until
   everyone else was ready to eat.
4 Although we looked everywhere, the cat was
   nowhere ....
5 Never .... Sweden for a holiday myself,
   I can't really say what it's like.
6 .... lead-free petrol becomes compulsory,
   the better it will be for all of us.

7 Had .... that dreadful traffic jam, we
   would have been here earlier.
8 So .... about the state of the city that he
   organised a protest demonstration.
9 Little .... that the woman I had insulted at
   the party was to be my lecturer on the ecology
   course the following term.
10 If they hadn't let that lovely old house become so
    dilapidated, ... to pull it down last
    month.

2 The second type of item is a simple dialogue exchange, with a blank in one half.
   Study this example:

---

②   ③

'Will you have another cup of tea?'

①   ①

'No, thank you. I've .... already.'

---

1 The 'have/'ve . . . already' tells you that the tense needed is Present
   Perfect.
2 The verb 'have' in the question suggests that the main verb needed in
   the answer is also 'have' i.e. 'have had', not 'have drunk/consumed/etc.'.
3 The phrase 'another cup of tea' tells you that the second speaker must
   have had at least one already, and possibly more. Therefore the
   speaker has probably had 'enough' or 'plenty' or 'more than enough',
   since he says 'No, thank you'.

Such reasoning then suggests that the sentence should read:
   'I've had enough/more than enough/plenty/one already.'

Now use the same kind of reasoning to fill in the blanks in these
exchanges with a suitable word or phrase.

1 'I've had terrible headaches for about a week now.'
   'Well, I think you'd .... and see a doctor about them.'
2 'Did you see the state of that lorry after it hit the wall?'
   'Yes. The driver must .... well over the speed limit.'
3 '........................ your driving test!'
   'Thank you very much. I thought I was bound to fail, but it's nice to be
   wrong.'
4 'Do you want me to read through the report before you send it off?'
   'Yes, I'd .... would.'
5 'What were all those people doing near the traffic lights when we
   passed?'
   'Oh, I think .... an accident. There was an ambulance there,
   too.'

Exam guidance

Complete the test exercises on this page before reading the opposite page.

SECTION A (Time: 30 minutes)

1 *Fill each of the numbered blanks in the following passage with* one *suitable word.*

The public's concern for captive animals is laudable, but, for the most part, misguided. They _____(1) ever, in fact, complain about the things in zoos _____(2) they should complain about, but they get vociferously hysterical _____(3) the things that do not matter a damn to the animal.

  People say that it is wrong to cage animals; it is _____(4) to imprison them; it is wrong to deprive them _____(5) their freedom. They seldom, _____(6) ever, criticise the cage; it is only the idea of the cage that they _____(7) to. The discovery _____(8) different animals have territories of different sorts and sizes, _____(9) from a few square feet to a few square miles, depending on the species, is a comparatively new _____(10).

---

2 *Finish each of the following sentences in such a way that it means exactly the same as the sentence printed before it.*

a) We must do something about the problem, even if it costs a lot. (Costly . . .)

b) They're constantly telling us what to do. (We . . .)

c) 'Our factory has never dumped waste into the local river,' the spokesman said. (The spokesman denied . . .)

d) They'll only do something about it when there's a major disaster. (Only . . .)

e) We should ban the use of pesticides, but we should also restrict the use of many other chemicals. (In addition . . .)

---

3 *Fill each of the numbered blanks with a suitable word or phrase.*

a) I wish .... to London with us. You would have enjoyed it.

b) By this time next year they .... in the same house for 25 years.

c) 'I was .... the way the film ended.'
   'Oh, I didn't find it that disappointing myself.'

d) John was .... gone to the conference, but he fell ill.

e) On .... information about the crime, the police inspector told reporters he would make a statement later.

---

4 *For each of the sentences below, write a new sentence as similar as possible in meaning to the original sentence, but using the words given: the words* must not be *altered* in any way.

a) She was humiliated by the whole experience. (**humiliating**)

b) You needn't attend the meeting if you don't want to. (**obligation**)

c) I'm extremely sorry I wasn't at the airport to meet you. (**apologies**)

d) A new law may soon be passed to deal with the problem. (**possibility**)

e) Many zoos are now breeding rare animals and birds very successfully in captivity. (**successful**)

ANSWERS

1
1. hardly/scarcely/never
2. which/that
3. about/over
4. wrong
5. of
6. if
7. object
8. that
9. ranging/varying/(going)
10. one

2
a) Costly as/though it may be, we must do something about the problem.
b) We are constantly being told what to do.
c) The spokesman denied (that) his/their factory had ever dumped . . ./denied his factory ever having dumped . . .
d) Only when there's a major disaster will they do something about it.
e) In addition to banning the use of pesticides, we should also restrict . . .

3
a) . . . (that) you had gone/travelled/come . . .
b) . . . will have lived/will have been/will have been living . . .
c) . . . (very/extremely) disappointed at/ by . . .
d) . . . (supposed) to have . . .
e) . . . being asked/pressed for (more/ further) . . .

4
a) She found the whole experience humiliating. OR The whole experience was humiliating for her.
b) You are under no obligation to attend the meeting.
c) Please accept my apologies for not being at the airport to meet you.
d) There is a possibility that a new law will soon be passed to deal with the problem.
e) Many zoos are now (being) very successful in/at breeding rare animals and birds in captivity.

EXPLANATIONS OF ANSWERS

1. Remember: *hardly/scarcely ever* = rarely.
2. Relative pronoun needed: NOT *who*.
3. *get hysterical about/over sthg*.
4. Rhetorical sentence, therefore *wrong* repeated.
5. *deprive sby of sthg*: NOT *from*. 6 *if ever*, meaning 'if they ever criticise'. 7 Note the verb *object to something*. 8 Conjunction *that* needed
9. *-ing* form needed with collocating verb.
10. The word *one* is needed to replace and refer back to *discovery*.

a) Remember the adjective structure *Difficult as/ though it is/may be, . . .*
b) Passive transformation, but note it is also in the Continuous form
c) Reported speech: *denied* is in the Simple Past, so 'has dumped' changes to *had dumped*
d) Inversion necessary (*will they do*) after *Only . . .*
e) Remember: *In addition to* + *-ing* form

a) Regret about past event, therefore *I wish you had done . . .*
b) *By* + future time requires *will have done/will have been doing*
c) The phrase 'that disappointing' is the clue to *disappointed (at/by)*
d) Remember: *be (supposed) to do/have done*
e) Remember: *On being asked* = *When he was asked*

a) Remember the different constructions needed with *-ed/-ing* adjectives.
b) *to be under (no/an) obligation to* = *(not) to have to*
c) The word is *apologies* (pl. n.), NOT *apologise* (vb.)
d) Remember the nouns *possibility, probability, need*, etc. to replace modal verbs. Collocation: *There is/was . . .*
e) Remember how differently adjectives and adverbs function. Watch prepositions: here, *successful at sthg*

Cover the opposite page and do this test exercise. Then read the opposite page.

SECTION B (Time: 45 minutes)

Read the following passage, then answer the questions which follow it.

Insects eat mummies in Peru's museums

Edward Schuhmacher, Lima

Pre-Columbian works of art and artifacts of major historical interest, some dating to 6,000 years before Christ, are rotting, crumbling or being stolen from museums
5 here.

Museum curators and archaeologists say that up to half of the priceless ceramics, textiles and other objects in Peru's more than 250 public and private museums have
10 been lost or irreparably damaged in recent years.

'Each day we are losing more,' says Senõr Luis Guillermo Lumbreras, a leading Peruvian archaeologist and former
15 director of the National Archaeology and Anthropology Museum. 'It's tragic.'

A Unesco study completed last month on Peru's museums concluded that after years of meagre budgets, they can no longer cope
20 with their problems.

The decay of antiquities is a problem shared by many developing nations, but Peru's problem is especially critical. Peru was one of the most advanced centres of
25 ancient civilisation in the Western hemisphere, and it holds an interest for museum curators, archaeologists and prehistorians matched only by Egypt and China.

The trouble began after objects were
30 removed from the ground and put in museums and storehouses without humidity controls.

Peru, which is one of the poorest nations in South America with a per capita income
35 of only about £600 a year, cannot afford the controlled environment that would assure the preservation of the relics.

A recent stockroom tour of the more than 500,000 pieces in the national
40 museum, an expanded farmhouse, showed them to be riddled with termites, infested with rats and attacked by fungi. The museum lacks climate controls and is seriously understaffed.

45 Many colourful painted ceramics have turned dull in storage. Among these are rows of 2,500-year-old Nazca polychrome vases depicting stylised cats and birds that are now faded and lifeless.

50 There are mummies in the museum, too. Peru's many ancient cultures – the Chavin, Paracas and Inca, which began emerging 8,000 years ago – mummified their dead and buried them with ceramics, weavings,
55 seeds and food.

While mummies thousands of years old have been exposed on storage shelves, insects have eaten the hair. Buckets of bare skulls sit in the courtyard outside. So do
60 soggy cardboard boxes where researchers keep their shards and other study pieces. The research takes place in wooden shacks.

a) What are museum curators and archaeologists in Peru so concerned about?
b) How are many museum pieces being 'lost'?
c) Why, apparently, has the state of Peru's museums come to light?
d) Explain the phrase 'years of meagre budgets' (ll.18–19).
e) Why is Peru's problem described as being 'especially critical'? (l.23)
f) What parallels are suggested between Peru, and China and Egypt?
g) What was one of the first causes of the decay of antiquities in Peruvian museums?
h) Explain the phrase 'a per capita income' (l.34).
i) In what ways are museum exhibits being attacked?
j) Explain the phrase 'turned dull in storage' (l.46).
k) Summarise in 50–100 words what the passage says about the state of affairs in Peru's museums at the time the article was written.

SUGGESTED OR POSSIBLE ANSWERS   EXPLANATIONS OF ANSWERS

a) The loss, disappearance or destruction of so many historical works of art or artifacts.

a) You need to read carefully and in effect summarise the information in paragraphs 1 and 2.

b) They are rotting, crumbling, being damaged or stolen.

b) The word 'lost' covers everything from decay to theft.

c) Because of a study carried out by Unesco.

c) Line 17 gives the information required.

d) Years in which financial allowances to the museums have been very small.

d) *meagre* = not enough in quantity e.g. *a meagre income/budget* etc.

e) Because its archaeology and pre-history is as important as that of Egypt and China.

e) From the reference given (l.23), the following lines explain why.

f) All three had advanced ancient civilisations and are therefore all of interest to archaeologists and historians.

f) The answer is to be found in ll.23–28.

g) They were never looked after properly after they had been dug up.

g) The answer is to be found in ll.29–32.

h) Average income for each person.

h) *per capita* = for or by each person.

i) They are being attacked by insects, rodents and fungus.

i) The answer is to be found in ll.38–44.

j) Lost their bright colours while they have been stored.

j) The phrase 'colourful painted ceramics' should help you here.

k) The summary, in a paragraph of your own wording, should contain these points:

1 $\frac{1}{2}$ of objects lost or damaged beyond repair.

2 More objects still being lost.

3 Peru cannot afford controlled environment necessary.

4 Lack of humidity controls.

5 Lack of climate controls and staff.

6 Works of art and artifacts rotting, infested with rats, etc.

EXAM ADVICE: General

1 Read all instructions on the Paper very carefully.

2 Watch the time! The time allowed for the whole Use of English Paper is **two hours**. We suggest you devote **approximately one hour to each Section of the Paper**.

Golden Rules for SECTION A

1 Read the instructions carefully and watch the time! Devote **no longer than 15 minutes** to any of the four test exercises. If you get stuck, go on to the next item.

2 *Test ex. 1:* Read the whole passage through for gist. Read the passage again and fill in the blanks. Always read beyond a blank to look for structural and other clues. Remember each blank requires ONE WORD ONLY. Think what *kind* of word is needed. Do not leave any blanks, even if you are unsure of your answers.

3 *Test ex. 2:* Work through the items one by one. Read each original sentence in detail and include all details in your rewritten version. Remember this is a test of grammar, so THINK! Again, do not leave any blanks.

4 *Test ex. 3:* Read each whole sentence or dialogue exchange to look for clues.

5 *Test ex. 4:* Remember: you MUST NOT CHANGE the word given.

Golden Rules for SECTION B

1 Read the instructions carefully, then read the whole passage for gist.

2 Read the last question (the summary) carefully, then re-read the passage, note the main points required for the summary (and possibly re-order them), and write the summary.

3 Then read the other questions and answer them. Remember to write short answers where possible.

4 Check the summary.

14 Leisure and Health

PAPER 4: LISTENING COMPREHENSION

With the increase in leisure time, certainly in the Western world, there is growing interest in all kinds of spare time activities, especially in personal fitness and health.

1 Find out about each other's pastimes. In pairs, ask each other the questions in this questionnaire.

Do you agree or disagree with this statement?
I do not have enough leisure time.

AGREE		DISAGREE	

Which of these things do you do in your spare time, and how often?

How often do you ...?	Every day	Once or twice a week	Once a month	Very rarely	Never
Read a book					
Watch TV					
Listen to the radio					
Play indoor games, e.g. cards, Monopoly, Scrabble, etc.					
Play video games					
Play outdoor games, e.g. tennis, football, golf, etc.					
Go swimming, or go for long walks					
Go to – the cinema – the theatre, opera or ballet – a concert – an art gallery, museum, etc.					
Play an instrument					
Play in an orchestra, pop group, etc.					
Sing (in a choir or a group)					
Go to the beach or to a lake					
Go fishing or hunting					
Go cycling, climbing, etc.					
Paint					
Attend a club, e.g. a youth club or some other organisation					
Help other people, e.g. the young, the elderly, the disabled, etc.					

Are there any other ways in which you _____
spend your leisure time which are not _____
mentioned above? If so, name them. _____

2 Now discuss your findings with the rest of the class.
Which seem to be the most popular pastimes? Which seem to be the least popular?

3 You are going to hear two people (a man and a woman) being interviewed in the street. As you listen, look at the questionnaire above and mark in their answers: 'M' for the man, 'W' for the woman. Then check your answers with the rest of the class.

Listening for mood, attitudes and feelings

In the Proficiency Paper 4 (Listening Comprehension) you may have to recognise different moods, attitudes, feelings and registers.

1 While they were speaking, the man and woman expressed certain moods, feelings and attitudes. Before you listen to parts of the interview again, look at the sentences below and listen to the way they express certain moods or feelings. On a piece of paper, write down the numbers 1–8 and, as you listen, write against each the mood, emotion or feeling you think is being expressed. The moods and feelings are:

IRONY or SARCASM   PAIN   DISAPPROVAL, ANNOYANCE or ANGER
SURPRISE   APPREHENSION or WORRY   ENTHUSIASM
BOREDOM or LACK OF INTEREST   DISGUST

1	Well, well! / Good heavens! / Phew! / Honestly? / Did you really?
2	Oh, I think it's wonderful! / Tennis is a great sport! / I can't think of anything better!
3	Ouch! (I've just cut my finger!) Phew! (I thought you said that wouldn't hurt!)
4	Ugh! / Yuk! (How can you eat that stuff?) Eeugh! (That looks awful!)
5	Well, I don't know . . . Oh, dear!
6	Mm, it's all right, I suppose, if you like that sort of thing. Well, I don't worry either way, really.
7	You might have *told* me! / I don't think that's funny at all! Would you please close the window! / He must have known, surely!
8	Oh, yeah! Fantastic! Opera? Oh, I *love* opera. I can't get enough of it.

Now check your answers with the rest of the class.

2 Now listen to parts of the interview with the man and woman again and answer these four multiple-choice questions. Discuss your answers afterwards.

1 When the man said 'But radio. Now that's different. I still think it's great . . .', he was

A sarcastic.
B bored.
C enthusiastic.
D angry.

2 The sound the man made just after his wife said 'Let me have a look' showed that he was

A very surprised.
B in pain.
C annoyed.
D full of interest.

3 When the man told the interviewer that he loved fishing, he was being

A honest.
B enthusiastic.
C disapproving.
D ironic.

4 By the time the man asked 'And how many more questions?',

A he was beginning to enjoy it.
B he was becoming pretty annoyed.
C he was in absolute agony.
D he was very very worried indeed.

3 Game: *Just a Minute* (see Teacher's Guide Unit 5)

Register: formal and informal

1 Read this extract from an article to find the explanation indicated in the title.

Why Exercise Makes You Slim

IN MY dieting days, I never knew whether my fatness was due to greed, sloth or the genes that I had inherited. The dieting books which I consumed provided no answer. Almost the only thing on which they agreed was that exercise could not help.

So, after more than a decade of dieting during which I had lost more than my own full weight, yet remained as fat as ever, I gave up. There seemed no point in torturing myself to so little effect.

A few months later, in the autumn of 1978, I took up jogging. It was going to Hyde Park to watch the first of the Sunday Times' series of National Fun Runs that got me interested. I was approaching 40, but the exaltation of the runners, some almost twice my age, was an inspiration. It wasn't that I expected to lose weight. The diet books had warned me that that was virtually impossible. But at least I might get fit, and if I didn't start immediately it would be too late.

By the following summer, I was doing gentle $4\frac{1}{2}$-mile runs and sometimes covered 20 miles in a week. Soon, I had shed 10 lb and was down to 12 stone. I have kept around this weight ever since, while at the same time eating and drinking whatever I wanted.

At first I regarded the weight loss as an enigma. Then I found other people who had enjoyed the same experience. It was when I realised I would never again have to diet that I started to investigate what had happened to me.

In theory, according to the diet books, exercise is not a particularly effective way of losing weight and fat. In practice, according to experience, exercise can be a most effective way of losing some weight and more fat.

Just as dieting slows you down, exercise, of the right type, speeds you up. Certain types of exercise including running, speed up the metabolic rate, not only while you exercise but also afterwards.

Thus, if you jog or run for 10 minutes, you burn 90 to 120 calories more than you would at rest, and you continue to burn more for some time. The extent to which the resting metabolic rate remains higher after exercise varies with the individual and the type of exercise.

2 Now listen to the way two people pass on the information contained in the article. One uses rather formal speech, the other rather informal speech.

When you have heard both, answer these questions and give reasons: Which was formal and which was informal? What sort of person would have said each, and in what situation?

3 Look at these characteristics of formal and informal speech. Then listen again and check which of them you hear on the tape.

Some characteristics of formal speech . . .

- full grammatical forms e.g. *I am not going to see her again.*
- noun constructions in place of verbs e.g. *The decision to do that was unwise.*
- full verbs in place of phrasal verbs e.g. *continue, discover, inflate,* etc.
- formal vocabulary in general e.g. *wise; a struggle; commence; become; employment*
- more precise vocabulary e.g. *a position, an appointment, a profession, a vocation*
- more complex language e.g. *I wonder if you would mind repeating that?* (for politeness and/or tact)
- use of conjunctions such as *thus, therefore, since, as, hence,* etc.

and informal speech

- shortened forms e.g. *I'm not going to see her again./I'm not gonna see . . .*
- simple verb constructions e.g. *It wasn't very clever to do that.*
- the frequent use of phrasal verbs e.g. *go on, find out, blow up,* etc.
- informal vocabulary in general e.g. *clever; a fight; begin; get; work*
- use of more general vocabulary e.g. *a job*
- simple sentences e.g. *Could you repeat that, please?*
- use of simple conjunctions such as *so, because,* etc.

Register: 'professional varieties' of English

Apart from the formal and informal registers of English, there are also
varieties used by people in different professions. This is the kind of
English used in the worlds of medicine, law, commerce, science, the arts,
the world of technology, and so on. Often such varieties involve little
more than a special set of vocabulary, but occasionally certain
grammatical constructions are favoured.

1 Many people in Britain and other
European countries are beginning to
fill some of their leisure time keeping
fit. In fact, quite an industry is growing
in Britain to cater for sports of all
kinds: it is said that there is 'wealth in
health'. Look at this photo and ask
and answer the questions in pairs.

1 What's happening in this photo? What
are the women doing, do you think?
Why?

2 How much does the caption tell you?
What does 'pounds' refer to as far as
a) Cindy Gilbert is concerned? and
b) 'the others' are concerned?

3 Do women in your own country attend
keep-fit (or aerobics) classes like this?
If so, how much do such classes cost,
and how many people go?
If not, why are there no such classes?
Would there be no interest?

4 What other kinds of sport are
becoming popular in your own country
(if any)?
If other sports *are* now becoming
popular, can you say why?
If they are not popular, can you say
why not?

*Housewives' choice: instructor Cindy Gilbert gains pounds
as others dance them away.*

2 Now listen to a small number of speakers talking about the subject of
Leisure and Health from the point of view of their own profession. As
you listen, put the number of the speaker against the profession. Then
check your answers with a partner.

A town planner   `6`   A doctor   `4`   A businessman   `8`

A sociologist   `2`   An arts counsellor `5`   A lawyer   `1`

3 Listen again and note down words and expressions related to each of
the professions.

Role play (see Teacher's Guide Unit 14)

Imagine there is a proposal to build a new 'Leisure Complex' in your
town or city. A meeting has been called to decide what interests need
to be catered for. Act out the meeting.

Exam guidance

Cover the bottom half of this page and do Part 1. Then read the comments below.

PART 1

🔊 *For questions 1–10 tick whether you think each is True or False, according to what you hear.*

	TRUE	FALSE	
1 The school holds classes for children and adults.			1
2 The method claims to teach *any* child to play the violin.			2
3 The school won't accept children under 7 years old.			3
4 Dr Suzuki's inspiration was children learning language.			4
5 Dr Suzuki applied his method to teaching all instruments.			5
6 Dr Suzuki does not play the violin himself.			6
7 When they begin, the children are immediately given a violin and bow.			7
8 Children are taught the correct posture before anything else.			8
9 The method implies total commitment by children and parents.			9
10 The speaker is convinced that children who join the school will *enjoy* the lessons there.			10

ANSWERS AND EXPLANATIONS OF ANSWERS

Note that the statements themselves, whether True or False, gave you a clear idea of the content of the talk: that it was about learning to play the violin, that Dr Suzuki was someone special, that you would probably hear about a 'method', etc.

1 **False**   Classes for children only. The speaker says: 'Many of you children will want to begin . . .'

2 **True**   The speaker says: '. . . every child is capable of becoming an accomplished violinist and musician.'

3 **False**   The speaker mentions 5- and 6-year-olds who will be playing later.

4 **True**   It was watching children learn language naturally and instinctively that led him to believe they could learn other things in the same way.

5 **False**   The speaker only mentioned 'learning to play the violin' (although the system may well now be applied to other instruments).

6 **False**   The speaker says that Dr Suzuki is 'a master' at the violin.

7 **False**   When they begin, the children are given 'toy violins and sticks for bows'.

8 **True**   The speaker talks about learning 'the correct violin-playing posture'.

9 **True**   Speaking to children and parents, the speaker says 'you can't go into this half-heartedly . . .'

10 **True**   The speaker says that children 'acquire immense enjoyment out of learning to play . . .'

Cover the bottom half of this page and do Part 2. Then read the comments below.

PART 2

For questions 11–24, listen and fill in the missing information.

Leisure

Table 114
Leisure activities by sex, 19___(11) Great Britain

percentage

	In full-time employment		Other[2]	
	Men	Women	Men	Women
Proportion in each category doing selected activity at least once in previous 4 weeks[1]				
A Home-based activities				
(13)_____	98	98	95	97
(14)_____	88	90	85	86
Gardening	___(15)	30	46	37
Hobbies	13	3	___(16)	3
Do-it-yourself	57	25	35	20
(12) **B**_____				
Total active_____(17)	52	39	___(18)	30
Total active indoor sports	___(19)	22	___(20)	10
Spectator sports	15	10	13	9
C Other leisure activities				
(24)_____	9	10	8	9
Visits to seaside	16	16	12	17
(21)_____	78	___(22)	53	___(23)
Going to bingo	5	11	5	11
Going to cinema/theatre	21	29	14	18
Total number of activities engaged at least once in previous 4 weeks (annual average)	8·9	8·4	7·1	7·3

[1] Annual average, except for outdoor activities and spectator sports, where percentages are based on the most popular (the summer) quarter.

[2] 'Other' includes those working part-time (less than 31 hours per week) and those not working at all.

ANSWERS

11 1977
12 Sporting activities
13 Watching television/TV
14 Listening to radio
15 50%
16 8%
17 Outdoor sports
18 35%
19 38%
20 12%
21 Going out for a meal/a drink
22 74%
23 51%
24 Visits to the countryside

COMMENTS

The table gave you a clear idea of what you were going to hear and what you would have to fill in or write as answers. You were obviously going to hear something about leisure activities in Britain. Then, by studying the table carefully, you should have realised that you would hear a lot of figures as percentages; and not only that, but you should have been able to predict how high or low some of the figures would be. Further, by reading the categories of leisure activities in the left-hand column, you should have been able to predict some of the missing information, particularly items 12 and 17, which almost *had to* be 'Sporting activities' and 'Outdoor sports' respectively. So the advice is: *read carefully in order to predict!*

Cover the opposite page and do Part 3. Then read the opposite page.

PART 3

🔊 *For questions 25–29, listen and for each tick one of the boxes A, B, C or D.*

25 When Mr James asked Mrs Skinner how her leg was,

A he was probably being polite. | A |

B he was genuinely concerned. | B |

C he was afraid she would sue the Club. | C |

D he thought he was speaking to someone else. | D |

26 How did Mrs Skinner break her leg?

A She fell during a game of tennis. | A |

B She fell down the Tennis Club steps. | B |

C She tripped over on her way to post the letter. | C |

D She fell down at home. | D |

27 One reason why Mrs Skinner rang Mr James was

A to complain about his letter. | A |

B to threaten him with legal action. | B |

C to demand a refund of her fees. | C |

D to discuss the coach's attitude to learners. | D |

28 When Mrs Skinner, at one point in the conversation, said 'Oh, thank you very much', she was being

A complimentary. | A |

B apprehensive. | B |

C grateful. | C |

D sarcastic. | D |

29 What reason did Mr James give for not agreeing to Mrs Skinner's request?

A She had not paid her entrance fee. | A |

B The Club brochure stated the situation clearly. | B |

C A solicitor had advised him he was right. | C |

D She still owed the Club £15. | D |

EXAM ADVICE: Ten golden rules for 'Listening Comprehension'

1 Read and listen to all instructions.

2 If you are in any doubt at all about what you have to do, ask the examiner or a monitor for further clarification.

3 *Don't* try to read through the whole Paper at the beginning. Read each Part as you are instructed.

4 Whatever you have to look at – multiple-choice items, true/false statements, a chart, a form, a map, a graph, etc. – read or study everything

very carefully in order to try to *predict* what you will hear!

5 Listen the first time and do as many of the items as you can. Listen the second time to check your answers or to fill in those you may have missed.

6 *Concentrate* during the listening phase. Remember, unlike Reading Comprehension, you can't glance back and forth to check for detail.

ANSWERS   EXPLANATIONS OF ANSWERS

25A	A Yes. He asked about her leg in a casual way and quickly cut short what she was saying by butting in with an 'Oh, good'. B No. While he was being polite, there was no indication that he was 'genuinely concerned'. His question was: 'How is your leg, by the way?' C No. He quite clearly had no worry that she might sue the Club. D No. He knew he was speaking to Mrs Skinner. She gave her name and he repeated it in 'Yes, I remember, Mrs Skinner'.
26D	A No. She only had one lesson: we don't even know if she played 'a game'. B No. There is no mention of the 'Tennis Club steps'. C No. She must have gone out to post the letter she sent to Mr James, but she didn't mention it. D Yes. She said: 'I broke my leg when I fell down some steps at home'.
27C	A No. She did complain that he had not replied, but she could not complain about his letter. B No. Although she suggested at the end that she would have to consult a solicitor, that was not the main reason for her call. C Yes. Quite simply, she wanted her money back. She had paid £30 for 15 lessons, of which she had only had the first one. D No. She said the (tennis) coach was excellent, but that again was not the reason she rang Mr James.
28D	After Mr James said 'We state quite categorically in our brochure, and you have a copy of it, that fees, once paid, are non-refundable', Mrs Skinner said 'Oh thank you very much!' At this point, she was being quite obviously sarcastic, since she had nothing to thank him for. (In the same way, the expression 'Thank you for nothing!' is heard in English when the speaker expresses annoyance and sarcasm.)
29B	A No. She *had* paid her entrance fee as part of the £30. B Yes. The situation was stated quite clearly/categorically in the brochure, and Mr James implied that Mrs Skinner should have read it. C No. There was no mention of Mr James having consulted a solicitor. It was Mrs Skinner who said she would have to consult a solicitor. D No. £15 was not mentioned. The only 'fifteen' mentioned was the number of lessons in the course.

7 Mark the answers on the answer sheet that you mean to. If you can do items 1 and 2, but not item 3, for example, remember to leave a gap for item 3 on your answer sheet when proceeding to item 4.

8 If you don't understand a word or phrase, don't agonise over it. What is meant may well become clear from the context, or it may even be explained later.

9 At the end, when checking through your answer sheet for the whole Paper, do not leave any gaps. Put in *something* for items you have left unmarked!

10 In the period leading up to the exam, listen to as much spoken English as you possibly can.

15 Aspects of Education

1 In small groups, tell each other about your education to date, for example: whether you went to a pre- or play school, what school you went to for primary education, what secondary education you had (or have had), and whether you have attended evening classes, or any further education.

At each stage of your discussion, give as much information as you can about a) the period you spent at a school, b) what the school was like – timetable, teaching, facilities for sport, etc., c) whether the school was segregated or co-educational, and d) what you thought of that period of your education.

2 Study this photo and then in pairs ask and answer the questions below, and discuss the general questions.

About the photo

1 How old do you think the children are?
2 Where are they, do you think? And who are the two women with them?
3 Do you think the children are enjoying the visit? Why?/Why not?

Personal

1 What might precede or follow such a visit? What would you do if you were a teacher? Why?

2 Do you remember going on any 'educational visits' when you were younger? What were they like?

For general discussion

The value of 'educational visits'.
Education in the future.
Discipline in schools and colleges.
The purpose of museums.

Reading aloud

Sentence stress

1 Read this text quickly and silently, then say what it is about, who could have written it and what it could be part of.

When the graduate goes home

When I finally went to university, I think the entire family was relieved. It was a respectable way – like marrying me off – of getting rid of me. When I then came back three years later, it was a shock to us all.

The worst thing about going to live at home after you have left university is that you are thrust back ten years in time. You finish university feeling suddenly grown up, as though the world's your oyster, only to find yourself back in your teens, living with your family again. And, if you're not careful, you can end up acting like a teenager.

For example, even though you're now 22, your parents will still feel free to criticise you occasionally. To tell you to do this or that and to tell you to do it now. Or to ask you where you've been, what you've been doing and who you've been doing it with. Teenagers can't take this sort of thing. They think they're too old. But at 22, you *are* too old. Being older you may try to listen to criticism, to see if it's fair – but you can still feel childishly hurt. This is unfair. You also tend to question why your parents are criticising you and to realise that criticism has a lot to do with putting people in their place, and keeping them under control. So you can feel the same irrational outrage the 13-year-old feels. Despite yourself, you hear yourself answering back. This does nothing for your self-esteem.

The second disturbing thing about going home as a graduate is that there can be a terrible sense of exclusion. After being a student for three years you don't have the same special place in the family as you did before. While at university, you may not have seen your family from one end of term to the next, keeping in touch only by telephone. On both sides there may have been a feeling of 'out of sight, out of mind', often to your mutual relief. Great domestic dramas could take place at home, with you being blissfully unaware. Momentous events could happen in your life too without your parents being involved. But this means you grow apart. Your family may even resent you coming back and being a reality again! They will have established ways of doing things. And if you don't like what you find, you won't be in a position to criticise or complain. There will be a certain amount of take it or leave it in their attitude to you. All of which can make you feel a little bit shut out.

Finally, if you are away for three years, relationships must change. While childhood relationships can be rooted in jealousy, rivalry, adoration, fear, dependence, or unconditional love, these are inappropriate feelings, when you grow up. You can't take anything for granted any more. The father-daughter, mother-daughter, brother-sister relationships – they all have to be redefined. You have to establish new relationships on an adult footing.

---

2 In English some words in a sentence are more stressed than others (i.e. they are pronounced more definitely). Listen to these sentences and mark the stressed words:

1 It was a respectable way – like marrying me off – of getting rid of me.
2 If you're not careful, you can end up acting like a teenager.
3 To tell you to do this or that and to tell you to do it now.
4 Teenagers can't take this sort of thing.
5 This does nothing for your self-esteem.
6 On both sides there may have been a feeling of 'out of sight, out of mind'.

Vocabulary items tend to be stressed: other words, such as articles, pronouns, prepositions, auxiliary verbs and demonstrative adjectives, do not, their vowels especially being shortened or even eliminated. Of course, any of these words can be stressed if the meaning requires it, for example:
She doesn't live here now. v *She DOES NOT live here now.* (Strong insistence)

3 Listen to the above sentences (1–6) again and repeat them.

4 Look at the final paragraph in the text above and mark those words you think should be stressed. Then check with a partner.

5 Listen to the final paragraph and check your predictions.

6 Listen to the same paragraph and repeat – sentence by sentence.

7 Mark the stressed words in the first paragraph and then practise reading it aloud to one another in pairs. Correct one another if necesary.

Preparing for the third phase of the Interview

In the third part of the Interview (described by the Cambridge Syndicate as a 'Structured Communication Exercise') you may have an individual or a small group interview with the examiner. This may take any one of a number of forms, such as discussion of a topic; an exposition of a topic; commenting on a newspaper article; giving advice about a problem; jigsaw reading; describing, interpreting and reacting to a painting; expanding on a newspaper headline; a role play; discussing solutions to a problem.

Here are some examples of Structured Communication Exercises and some advice on how to approach them.

1 Individual exposition of a topic

You may be asked to talk for a minute or two on a topic. If you are, you may have time to prepare it briefly. We suggest you plan it very much like a short composition: in other words, jot down some ideas in note form (together with some vocabulary) and then re-order them ready to speak.

Look at this topic and the ideas, then talk about it for a minute or two. Add your own ideas as you think fit:

Topic

The effect of the technological revolution on traditonal forms of education

Ideas

- increasing use of computers in schools, colleges, etc.
- some students in Europe now have computers at home: effect?
- use of computers for self-study (or individual study) at school
- less time spent in class groups in future? more time spent studying on one's own or with students of other ages but similar interests and studies?

Now study these topics, make notes and be prepared to talk on one of them for a minute or so:

1 Memories of my early education
2 What school has done for me
3 The ideal education system
4 Subjects I wish I had studied at school
5 Parents and teachers should consult more on children's education

2 Discussion with the examiner

The examiner may discuss a topic with you.
Imagine you are given this topic: 'Co-educational vs segregated schools'. As in **1** above, jot down some brief notes, then compare your ideas with another student and discuss this issue by putting forward ideas, countering them, interrupting where necessary, asking for examples or clarification, etc.

3 Expanding on a newspaper headline

You may be asked to try to explain the possible background to a newspaper headline. Imagine you are given this headline: 'FISH INVADE HOLIDAY RESORT'. Think of all the possible events that could lead to this headline. Could it be pollution, for example, or a freak of nature, dumping of fish by fishermen, or even some kind of Carnival joke? Quickly jot down the outline of your ideas, then explain what you think to a partner and say how each state of affairs might have come about.

4 Giving advice about a problem

You may be given an outline of a problem situation either in the form
of a short text or in the form of a visual and text combined
(as below). First of all, study the problem situation carefully to make
sure you fully understand all aspects of it, and then think yourself into
the situation so that it becomes real to you. Once you have done that,
the advice you are required to give should come automatically.
Imagine you are given the following:

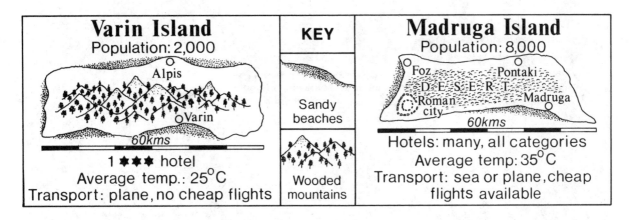

Find out from the examiner what his/her preferences are for a holiday
destination, then advise which island to visit, giving reasons.

Think what the possible attractions and disadvantages of each island
could be for people with a range of different tastes and interests, then
ask questions accordingly. Once you have established what the
examiner seems to like, you can begin to give advice. Practise doing
this with different students in the class.

5 Role play in a group situation

You may be asked to take part in a role play as a member of a small
group working from role descriptions as below or from information
about a particular situation. In groups of five, study this role play and
the descriptions of the participants and their points of view. Then
discuss education in society today, each taking one of the roles below:

Education in society today

A university lecturer, who feels the primary aim of education is the
acquisition of knowledge

An industrialist, who thinks education should train students for a future
job or profession (i.e. acquisition of skills)

A parent, who is of the opinion that education should equip young
people to become responsible citizens, ready to play their part in
society (i.e. a general, all-round education)

A person who believes that the best form of education is through work
itself from an early age.

A parent who wants to educate his or her own children (and not in fact
send them to school).

Exam guidance

1 Picture conversation

a) Study this photo carefully and then in pairs ask and answer the questions below.

1 Where and when do you think this photo was (or might have been) taken? Why?
2 Do you think these people look ridiculous? Why?/Why not?
3 Do you know, or can you guess, why they are wearing 'bubbles' on their heads?
4 All of them suffer from hay fever, and the bubble allows them to breathe pollen-free air. If you suffered badly from hay fever, would you wear one of these? Why?/Why not?

Now write down more questions that might be asked about the photo, and then again in pairs ask and answer them.

b) General questions and topics for discussion.
In pairs, ask each other these questions and continue each as a general discussion.
1 What other common ailments or diseases do we still need to find cures for?
2 When they were first invented, many common everyday gadgets, machines and so on looked very strange. Can you think of any? What did they look like, and what do they look like now?

EXAM ADVICE for the Picture Conversation

1 When you are handed the picture, study it very carefully, noting the details – situation, actions, clothes, objects, facial expressions, etc. Think of the language you need in order to describe what is happening, etc.

2 While studying the photo, think of questions that *you* could ask someone about it. In the Interview, you will only see the photo: you will not *see* the questions. So be prepared for a range of questions from purely factual correctness to hypothesising, and try to think of related general questions and discussion topics which might arise from the photo.

3 Right from the start of the Interview, communicate! In other words, don't give short one- or two-word answers; be prepared to elaborate. And *don't mumble*: speak as clearly as you can.

4 Remember to ask for a repetition or clarification if you don't understand what the examiner says.

5 Don't be afraid to express ignorance or make assumptions about what is happening in the picture. The photo is intended merely as a prompt to conversation, not as a test of your ability to understand photos.

6 Express your views on the related topics honestly, and give reasons for your opinions.

2 Reading passage

Study each of these short passages and be prepared to read one of them aloud. Before you read each passage aloud, you must identify the probable speech situation, in other words say who said it to whom, in what kind of situation and why, etc.

a)
> I suspect that it's almost too late to do anything at all constructive about some of our conservation problems. With one or two eminent colleagues, I have recently undertaken the conduct of a large research programme into the effects of heavy traffic on ancient buildings in just one city in Europe. Our early findings are frightening. In so many ways, we are simply abusing our environment.

b)
> Of course many of us read science fiction. Strangely enough, it's one of the ways many of us get ideas for future projects. I know that if I hadn't read a certain short story by Brian Aldiss – you know, the science fiction writer – a couple of years ago, I wouldn't be doing the work I'm doing now. I've rarely found a practical, scientific solution in any science fiction, but there are always ideas there to set you thinking.

c)
> The moment the witness stood up in the box and denied ever having met my client, I knew I had the case won. All I could really do was to congratulate the prosecution for putting a witness in the box for my benefit. Everything else suggested that my client was guilty, and he would have got ten years, I would think, but what the witness said saved the day.

EXAM ADVICE for the Reading Passage

1 Read the passage you are given silently right through to see what it is about and to decide who might have said it, etc.

2 Study it more carefully in order to prepare to read it aloud: here you must remember punctuation, pronunciation, word and sentence stress, and intonation.

3 When asked to read the passage, read it as clearly and as meaningfully as you can, but in a relaxed manner so that it sounds as natural as you can make it. (And remember, if the passage includes contracted forms e.g. *I'm, they'll, we're*, etc., read them as contracted forms, NOT full forms *I am, they will, we are*, etc.)

3 Structured communication exercise

Since the examiner will be looking for a candidate's ability to function in a serious discussion or seminar at Proficiency level, this third part of the Interview (whatever form it may take) allows for freer discussion.

a) Imagine you are given this topic to discuss or to give a short talk on: 'Keeping fit'.

Here are some ideas and notes
you might make:

1 Important to keep fit – enjoy life more.
2 Keeping fit – not only physically, but mentally. And balanced diet (no smoking or drinking) and regular habits.
3 Sports of all kinds – individual and group: jogging, swimming, tennis, football, etc.
4 More facilities now – e.g. keep-fit and aerobics classes for all ages.
5 Myself – swimming and sailing.

Now make brief notes and be prepared to talk for a minute or so on them or to discuss them:
1 Space travel 2 Mind over Matter 3 The value of zoos
4 An unforgettable experience 5 Preserving the environment

b) Imagine the examiner initiates a discussion on the media, its aims and responsibilities. You are asked to talk briefly on the subject as 1 a newspaper reporter; 2 a television programme producer; 3 a parent of three or four children; 4 an elderly person (who is a grandparent); 5 a producer of radio current affairs programmes. In groups of five, discuss the aims and responsibilities of the media in today's world (radio, television and newspapers). Each student in the group should make notes in order to speak as e.g. the newspaper reporter, and so on.

EXAM ADVICE for the Structured Communication Exercise

1 When given preparation time, make *brief notes* only – three or four ideas and perhaps some useful vocabulary items.

2 Be prepared to *take part*. In other words, don't simply answer questions or just read your notes. Your notes are meant to be prompts only. Be prepared to ask questions yourself, to elaborate on what you say and to give clear examples of what you mean.

3 Try to imagine yourself fully into any situation or role you may be given.

GENERAL EXAM ADVICE for the whole interview

1 Be as confident as you can, be forthcoming, and relax!

2 Remember: above all, the examiner is trying to find out *how well you can speak English*; he or she can only do this if you are prepared to talk.

Proficiency Practice Exam

PAPER 1   READING COMPREHENSION   (Time: 1 hour)

This Paper is in two parts, Section A and Section B. For each question you answer correctly in Section A you gain one mark; for each question you answer correctly in Section B you gain two marks. No marks are deducted for wrong answers.
Answer all the questions. Indicate your choice of answer in every case on a separate sheet (which in the examination should show your name and examination index number). Follow carefully the instructions about how to record your answers.

SECTION A

In this Section you must choose the word or phrase which best completes each sentence. For each question, 1 to 25, indicate on your answer sheet the letter A, B, C or D against the number of the question.

1 The accident .... the train's departure by a few hours.
   A retained   B sent back   C delayed   D called off

2 The sound of a tap .... stopped him going to sleep.
   A squirting   B dripping   C splashing   D slopping

3 Before the firm closed down, it made 200 workers ....
   A obsolete   B unemployed   C redundant   D extra

4 The manager asked his secretary to take .... of the meeting as it progressed.
   A records   B note   C reports   D minutes

5 Hardly a single old building .... standing after the council remodelled the town.
   A remained   B stayed   C kept   D continued

6 The precious crystal vase .... into a thousand pieces when it hit the floor.
   A crumpled   B dashed   C splintered   D crushed

7 They couldn't decide what to do so they .... a coin.
   A flung   B threw   C spun   D tossed

8 After much fruitless discussion the meeting was .... to the following day.
   A adjourned   B deferred   C held up   D withheld

9 The old man sat in a corner quietly .... a song to himself as he waited.
   A cooing   B gurgling   C croaking   D humming

10 The food being cooked in the kitchen was giving .... a wonderful smell.
   A up   B off   C round   D over

11 The journalist was in a .... as to what to do for the best.
   A quandary   B puzzle   C predicament   D contradiction

12 She spends a .... deal of her time at work.
   A large   B high   C great   D big

13 At first he was somewhat .... by the amount of responsibility the new job involved.
   A daunted   B abashed   C agog   D surpassed

14 The light was so .... that for a few minutes they couldn't see anything.
   A dazzling   B glinting   C glimmering   D sparkling

15 The doctor told him that the .... he would gain from a healthy diet would be well worth the sacrifice.
   A profits   B benefits   C advantages   D welfare

16 The judge .... them to two years in prison.
   A prosecuted   B sentenced   C convicted   D accused

17 At the supermarket he was handed a .... with all the week's bargains and prices.
   A booklet   B leaflet   C supplement   D prospectus

18 They were .... upset by the news.
   A utterly   B strongly   C extremely   D absolutely

19 The manager said there was a slim .... of business improving within the next year.
   A likelihood   B prospect   C horizon   D perspective

20 The party was suddenly interrupted by a .... scream.
   A stabbing   B strident   C shrieking   D piercing

21 The .... down the side of the street were full of dead leaves and rubbish.
   A channels   B gutters   C ditches   D ducts

22 The car comes with a guarantee. .... , it's still necessary to take out insurance.
   A Notwithstanding   B Besides   C However   D Thus

23 They couldn't decide what measures .... be taken.
   A should   B needed   C need   D ought

24 The wound in his leg took a long time to ....
   A heal   B mend   C cure   D treat

25 The city authorities decided to .... many of the city's old buildings.
   A rectify   B reconstitute   C restore   D recondition

SECTION B

In this Section you will find after each of the passages a number of questions or unfinished statements about the passage, each with four suggested answers or ways of finishing. You must choose the one which you think fits best. For each question, 26 to 40, indicate on your answer sheet the letter A, B, C or D against the number of the question.

FIRST PASSAGE

As with every artistic movement, it is necessary to examine the style against which it rebelled in order fully to understand it. Stanislavsky and Chekhov cannot be entirely appreciated without being at least conscious of the melodramatic style of acting against which they reacted. The husband, finding love-letters from another man to his wife, would stagger back a couple of paces unsteadily and raise his hand to his forehead as though warding off one of destiny's blows. 'Life', affirmed Chekhov, 'is not like that', a sentiment faithfully echoed by Stanislavsky. A man finding such letters usually does not react at all, at least visibly. His immediate concern is to try to capture a kind of diabolical initiative by leaving the letters exactly as he found them so that he has all the time in the world to study his quarry and to decide on his reaction. After all, he doesn't wish an accusation of snooping to lessen his moral ascendancy.

Naturally each man would have his own reaction to such a situation as would each theatrical character, but what both Chekhov and Stanislavsky were sure of was that only a ham actor, obeying the instructions of a conventional dramatist and a workaday director, could totter back the statutory two steps and bring his left hand up to his eyebrow. Chekhov thereupon set about showing up the false by a poetic mobilisation of all that is inconsequential and wayward in human intercourse, with the result that his plays are not so much dialogues as many intertwined monologues, plays in which people talk far more than they listen.

Since Chekhov, the journeys into the depths of realism and beyond have been accomplished more thoroughly if not more profoundly by the cinema, but the theatre is the one dramatic art-form left which exploits a living audience, as does a sport. I submit today, as I have always submitted, that the theatre is basically a sport, based on integrated team-play, with, as in all sports, room for improvisation and the opportunities of the moment, and very much dependent on physical and vocal condition. The driver of a racing-car maintains a loose grip on the steering-wheel, and uses it merely to correct the car when an emergency looms. The rest of the time, he 'feels' his car round the course. So it is with acting. The mental processes are too fast to intellectualise at every curve in the road, and grip the steering-wheel as though your life depended on it.

26   According to the passage, Stanislavsky and Chekhov
  A   were similar.
  B   knew one another.
  C   saw acting in a similar way.
  D   are difficult to appreciate immediately.

27   The passage tells us that usually in real life men finding love letters addressed to their wives
  A   plot revenge.
  B   behave diabolically.
  C   risk being considered immoral.
  D   play for time and don't react visibly.

28 Chekov and Stanislavsky believed that
 (A) ham actors obey instructions well.
 B ham actors control their movements well.
 C actors and real people react similarly.
 D melodramatic styles of acting are unrealistic.

29 Chekhov's plays are characterised by
 (A) monologues.
 B hypocritical conversations.
 C a lack of dialogues.
 D little genuine dialogue.

30 The author believes that theatre
 A has been taken over by cinema these days.
 (B) has become merely another sport.
 C has lost its impetus.
 D shares the characteristics of sport.

31 According to the author, actors
 A must be flexible.
 (B) can easily lose their grip.
 C face many risks.
 D must play their parts with determination.

SECOND PASSAGE

It is a paradox that man has tended from the earliest times to dispose of his wastes in the water courses from which much of his drinking water is to come. But under natural conditions, rivers have very considerable powers of self-cleansing. The flow of water scours the detritus – of salt and soil and sticks and stone – out to the oceans. Bacteria use the oxygen dissolved in the water to decompose organic wastes and in turn are consumed by fish and water plants who return oxygen and carbon to the biosphere. The only real risk under these simple conditions is that some of the minute bacteria will get into someone's drinking water and give him one of the very large range of intestinal diseases which over the millenia have been a major human scourge. This remains the principal pollution in most of the world and is increasing with rising population.

But as mankind enters the new urban-industrial order, the problem of waterborne wastes becomes much more complicated. First of all, industry brings thousands upon thousands of people together in urban concentrations. 'Natural' systems of sewage disposal down the rivers become grossly overloaded. Then industrial processes can very greatly increase the range of materials which bacteria cannot deal with (the non-biodegradable kind) – and some of them are poisons, particularly compounds like cyanides or minerals like mercury and lead. These, piled in industrial tips over the landscape may also, by seepage, release their poisons into underground waters or neighbouring streams.

Then again, even the organic (or bio-degradable) wastes – from municipal sewage, from pulp and paper-making – can overload the river's available supplies of dissolved oxygen. The bacteria use it all up as they decompose the sewage. Oxygen levels fall. Sometimes there is simply none left and, since all aquatic life requires oxygen, the river loses its capacity of carrying living things and may flow on for miles as a dead and stinking sewer. The slower the river's flow, the greater is the risk.

32 According to the passage the main source of water pollution is
  A natural systems of sewage disposal down rivers.
  B sewage in urban concentrations.
  C seepage from industrial tips.
  D industrial waste.

33 The passage tells us that bacteria in river water
  A make millions of people ill every year.
  B cannot break down all waste matter.
  C are destroyed by industrial waste.
  D absorb too much oxygen.

34 According to the passage the new urban-industrial order
  A poisons rivers and streams.
  B damages the natural life cycle of rivers.
  C has led to an increase in population.
  D has totally destroyed the natural systems of sewage disposal.

35 The passage tells us that the disposal of waterborne wastes becomes complicated in urban-industrial areas because of
  A too much sewage.
  B bio-degradable waste.
  C a combination of factors.
  D non-biodegradable wastes.

THIRD PASSAGE

Extract 1
You can get retirement pension when
● you reach pension age and
● you have retired, or can be treated as retired, from regular employment.
But, if you're a woman who is widowed when over 60, you can get a retirement pension on your late husband's contributions whether or not you have retired.

You are treated as having retired if:
● you are not doing any paid work;
or
● you carry on with some paid work.

Extract 2
Like many a successful person, you will be aware that one of your greatest financial assets is the ability to earn a high income. You will also be aware that the possibility of a comfortable retirement is likely to be adversely affected by the combination of a reduced income and the ever-increasing cost of living.

Quite apart from retirement, you may well wish to accumulate some capital to give you some financial 'elbow room' in the years ahead.

Three main obstacles conspire to reduce the effectiveness of creating capital out of income . . .

Extract 3

The government's decision to pay the increase in two stages – on 1 August 1983 and
1 January 1984 – means the full pay increase will not be effective for pension purposes until
next year.

Members whose pensions become due for payment between April 1983 and January
1984 'will suffer a permanent penalty which cannot be recouped', says the CSSU. They will
have left the service before receiving the total pay increase to which they are entitled with no
subsequent reassessment of their position.

Officers retiring between April and August 1983 stand to lose out completely if the
Treasury refuses to reconsider its decision.

36 Which of these statements about the three extracts is true?
    A   They probably all come from the same newspaper article.
    B   They are all selling a particular pension scheme.
    C   They are probably taken from three different sources.
    D   They contradict one another.

37 As far as the style of the extracts is concerned which is true?
    A   The first is the most personal.
    B   The second is advertising language.
    C   The third is relaxed and chatty.
    D   None is direct and staightforward.

38 The three extracts are concerned with
    A   setting up pension schemes.
    B   claiming pension payments.
    C   complaining about pension schemes.
    D   schemes for financial provision later on in life.

39 The third extract is
    A   purely factual.
    B   subjective.
    C   a mixture of fact and opinion.
    D   propaganda.

40 We can conclude from all three extracts that
    A   you need capital to get a pension.
    B   you can work even if you're retired.
    C   retirement entitles you to a comfortable pension.
    D   people's income after retirement can vary according to circumstances.

PAPER 2   COMPOSITION   (Time: 2 hours)

Write two only of the following composition exercises. Your answers must follow exactly the instructions given. Write in pen, not pencil. You are allowed to make alterations, but see that your work is clear and easy to read.

1   Describe the city that has made the greatest impression on you. (About 350 words)

2   Parents and school should play equal parts in a child's education and upbringing. Discuss. You may write in the form of a dialogue between two speakers, or in essay form. (About 350 words)

3   Describe and discuss the environmental problems of the place where you live as well as any possible solutions. (About 250 words)

4   Below is a TV guide showing what's on tonight.

6.30 – 7.10	International Boxing
7.10 – 7.25	News
7.25 – 7.30	Weather forecast
7.30 – 8.45	Crime In Our Cities (a documentary on the violence of life in urban environments)
8.45 – 10.00	Miss World (Which country's fabulous beauty will win this year's fabulous prize?)
10.00 – 10.50	Scotch Whisky (a report on Scotland's finest brew – who makes it, where and how)
10.50 – 11.05	Late night news

You have just read it through with horror. It seems to you that TV programmes have been getting worse and worse lately, and tonight's are just the limit. You and your family will not be watching them as you find them objectionable to you personally and potentially harmful to your children.
Write an angry letter of protest to the manager of your local TV station stating your position, giving reasons for your disgust and adding anything else you may wish. Your answer should not exceed 200 words.

PAPER 3   USE OF ENGLISH   (Time: 2 hours)

SECTION A

1   *Fill each of the numbered blanks in the following passage with* one *suitable word.*

Not once in my life, living ......*where*...... (1) I always have in one of England's few

truly mountainous areas widely renowned ......*seen*...... (2) its wild beauty,

......*as*...... (3) I imagine that news ......*from*...... (4) the outside world would

easily shake or concern me – but this did. I am an easy-going, good-natured fellow

......*warm*...... (5) heart, and one not lightly moved, ...*so*...... (6) the

pronouncement by the world's media that ......*one*...... (7) of my fellow men had

indeed set foot ......*on*...... (8) Mars, the 'Red Planet', filled me ......*with*...... (9)

an emotion not far short of elation. Hardly daring to believe ......*what*...... (10) I had

read, I stumbled out of my crofter's cottage to stand and gaze up ......*into*...... (11) the

night sky. Whichever pinpoint of light was Mars, ...*there*...... (12) they were, these

men who ......*had*...... (13) been prepared if necessary to sacrifice themselves, not

......*for*...... (14) their families or their country, ...*as*...... (15) had millions

before them ......*known*...... (16) history in the causes of freedom and justice,

......*but*...... (17) for mankind and the advancement of his knowledge

......*of*...... (18) the universe. If anyone ......*had*...... (19) told me that I would

witness ......*such*...... (20) an event in my short lifetime, I would have said they were

mad.

PRACTICE EXAM: PAPER 3

2 Finish each of the following sentences in such a way that it means exactly the same as the sentence printed before it.

EXAMPLE: They're pulling down the old church.

ANSWER: The old church *is being pulled down.*

a) Even though the weather wasn't very promising, we still went to the beach.

In spite of _not promising weather we went to the beach_

b) Because of her accident she couldn't ride for six months.

Her accident _unable her to ride for 6 months_

c) She broke down the moment she heard the news.

On _the hearing the news he broke down_

d) I had just left the house when I heard the phone ring.

No sooner _I heard the phone ring then when I just left the house_

e) He's very strong, but he still can't lift that box.

Strong _man still can't lift that box_

f) I'm sure he was having a bath when I called.

He must _have had a bath when I called_

g) Please don't ask her to the party.

I'd rather _you too didn't ask her to the_

h) John is the most dedicated singer there is in the choir.

There isn't _more dedicated singer than John is in the choir_

3 Fill each of the numbered blanks with a suitable word or phrase.

EXAMPLE: He took his car to the garage _to have it_ repaired.

a) It's too late now that the holiday's over, but I wish _we had gone_ somewhere else.

b) You _should have_ your eyes tested a long time ago.

c) 'How long have you known Jim?'

'Oh, I _he known_ in Paris ten years ago.'

d) 'I think we should try that new restaurant on Saturday night.'

'Yes, ~~I've thought about it~~, too.'

e) 'Look. This is how I solved the problem.'

'That's interesting. I ~~ve solved it~~ completely differently.'

f) ~~The more~~ I try to help him, the less he listens.

4 *For each of the sentences below, write a new sentence as similar as possible in meaning to the original sentence, but using the words given: these words must not be altered in any way.*

EXAMPLE: I assumed without asking that they'd be at the meeting.

took

ANSWER: *I took it for granted that they'd be at the meeting.*

a) The concert wasn't as good as we had expected.
expectations

~~Our expectations were much higher about the concert than the concert itself~~

b) He advised me to rest for a month.
advice

~~The advice he gave was to rest for a month~~

c) He managed to get the job finished because his secretary was so efficient.
thanks

~~Thanks to his efficient secretary he managed..~~

d) After the book, the film was a terrible letdown.
disappointing

~~After the book, the film was a very disappointing~~

e) Somehow his hand was crushed in the car door.
had

~~He had his hand crushed in the car door~~

f) He can hardly see at all without glasses.
practically

~~He practically can't see without~~

g) I wish you weren't going on that trip.
rather

~~I'd rather you didn't go on that trip.~~

h) People believe that she was born in Australia.
believed

~~She is believed to be born in Australia~~

125

SECTION B

5   *Read the following passage, then answer the questions which follow it.*

New waves of invaders are sweeping across Europe. Fortunately their intentions are not warlike; they are merely seeking to make good use of their holiday or weekend leisure-time. All the same, they are creating a considerable stir: the treasure-hunters are coming, the treasure-hunters are here!

Armed with increasingly sophisticated metal-detectors, they sally forth at the crack of   5
dawn to track down Celtic coins, Merovingian clasps or Gallo-Roman bronzes. Off they go on their searches and – scandalously enough – they often find something!

Indeed, they find a lot, much too much for the liking of official archaeologists who are beginning to get worried, especially as the ranks of the treasure-hunters are swelling rapidly.   10

It was therefore high time for the European parliamentarians to seek legislative arrangements aimed at protecting national heritages without seriously encroaching on the freedom of the treasure-hunters whose activities are far from being purely negative.

With a view to this, work began on a Parliamentary Assembly report on metal-detectors and archaeology, and an initial parliamentary hearing was held in Paris on   15
5 December 1980. This hearing was attended by archaeologists and representatives of detector manufacturers and users. In the light of the views expressed by each side it is already possible to form an idea of the main arguments for or against treasure-hunting. Among the major accusations against treasure-hunters, there is first of all the charge that they cause damage to listed archaeological sites by taking away the objects they contain   20
and irreparably disrupting the pattern of evidence of the past. Archaeologists feel that participation by non-specialists is extremely harmful and that it would be better not to excavate at all than to do so inexpertly. But that is not all. In view of the number and value of the finds (e.g. the discovery of the Tipperary Chalice in Ireland), archaeologists hold that treasure-hunters have no right to excavate, considering it immoral that they should   25
keep their finds and accusing them of engaging in what amounts to nothing less than plundering the collective heritage of the past. This implies that not only should deep excavations be prohibited but also the picking-up of objects just under the surface, if it is agreed that in archaeological terms even the surface tells a story.

A final argument which is not without significance is that archaeologists would soon   30
be overwhelmed owing to lack of numbers if all supposedly well-meaning amateurs were to bring them all their finds.

In general, the treasure-hunters proclaim their right to a healthy leisure-time activity which has the advantage of combining culture and non-violent sport. They also point to the usefulness of their hobby by stressing the importance of certain discoveries which   35
would not have been made but for them, and thus try to justify the role played by the amateur archaeologists as auxiliaries to professionals.

They also claim that the usefulness of the detector cannot be questioned as official excavators use it themselves on certain sites. They vociferously maintain that the lucrative aspect of a treasure-hunt is of secondary importance by comparison with its   40
archaeological interest, and they fail to see why a passion for the past should be the sole prerogative of official archaeologists.

Lastly, they put forward two technical arguments which seem relevant: one concerns the scientific value of recording isolated finds (which could not have been made otherwise, since the recognised experts are too busy with their work on listed sites); the other is that it is desirable to dig up buried metal objects without delay because their survival is seriously threatened by the widespread use of fertilisers and pesticides.   45

a)   Why are the treasure-hunters described as 'invaders' (1.1)?

b)   What picture does the writer try to evoke by saying that the treasure-hunters 'sally forth at the crack of dawn' (11.5–6)?

c)   Explain the phrase 'the ranks . . . are swelling' (1.9).

d)   What was the European Parliamentary investigation set up to do?

e)   What word(s) or phrase(s) might make you think that the writer has some sympathy with treasure-hunters who use metal-detectors?

f)   What was the purpose of the hearing held in Paris in December 1980?

g)   Explain the phrase 'listed archaeological sites' (1.20).

h)   Why does it worry the archaeologists that treasure-hunters have made so many and such valuable finds?

i)   What is the relevance of the phrase 'even the surface tells a story' (1.29)?

j)   How can official archaeologists be said to have a 'lack of numbers' (1.31)? ·

k)   Explain the meaning of the phrase 'but for them' (1.36)?

l)   Explain the phrase 'they vociferously maintain' (1.39).

m) How interested do treasure-hunters claim to be in making money from their activities?

n)   In what way could official archaeologists be said to possess the sole prerogative to have a passion for the past (11.41–42)?

o)   In one paragraph of 50–100 words, summarise the arguments put forward by treasure-hunters in defence of their activities.

PAPER 4   LISTENING COMPREHENSION   (Time: 20–30 minutes)

FIRST PART

For questions 1–10, fill in the missing information or tick ($\sqrt{}$) the boxes as appropriate.

Ring the 'All-Office' Secretarial College!

Find out — about the courses

① when the next general office course
starts for beginners: _Mon 16th May_

② how long it lasts: _12 weeks_

③ from _16th May_ to _8th August_

④ how many hours you have a day: _5_

⑤ if classes are mixed: YES $\boxed{\sqrt{}}$ NO $\boxed{}$

⑥ how much the course costs: _£400_

⑦ if you can pay in instalments YES $\boxed{\sqrt{}}$ NO $\boxed{}$

⑧ if they can provide accommodation —
in the college $\boxed{}$ or with a family $\boxed{\sqrt{}}$

⑨ how much it would cost (per week) for
just bed and breakfast: _15-20£ per week_

⑩ or bed, breakfast and evening meal:
£25 per week

SECOND PART

For each of questions 11–16 put a tick in one of the boxes, A, B, C or D.

11 From the host's introductions we know that two of the panel

    A   attended Hightown Polytechnic.

    B   are active members of the Animal Rights movement.

    C   were born and raised in the Hightown area.

    D   write a weekly column for the 'Daily News'.

A
B
C
D

12 James Smith voted against the proposal in parliament because

    A   he owns a goods haulage firm himself.

    B   he only agrees with juggernauts on motorways.

    C   he thinks transport costs must be kept down.

    D   he is more concerned with transport than with our heritage.

A
B
C
D

13 Joan Hunter would like to see the size and speed of vehicles reduced

    A   in order to save lives.

    B   until our country roads can be improved.

    C   because she is concerned with Human Rights.

    D   before there is no room left on roads to travel on.

A
B
C
D

14 In order to stop juggernauts, Jeremy Slade suggests that

    A   you have to become a town councillor.

    B   you may have to take drastic action.

    C   you have to support old buildings.

    D   you need to pass local laws.

A
B
C
D

15 According to Claire Cook, the world would be a better place

    A   if we all walked and cycled everywhere.

    B   with more public transport.

    C   if it followed the panel's advice.

    D   without petrol-driven vehicles.

A
B
C
D

16 What opinion do all four panelists have?

    A   They have the same objections to juggernauts. | A |

    B   They believe juggernauts should be banned completely. | B |

    C   They think juggernauts should be restricted to motorways. | C |

    D   They object to juggernauts for one reason or another. | D |

THIRD PART

For each of questions 17–22 put a tick in one of the boxes A, B, C or D.

17 What did the author say about Fotheringay's miraculous powers?

    A   They revealed themselves unexpectedly. | A ✓ | ✓

    B   They were due to his strong imagination. | B |

    C   They were innate. | C |

    D   They could have been predicted. | D |

18 Toddy Beamish kept saying 'So you say'

    A   to express his agreement. | A ◀ |

    B   to show that he understood. | B |

    C   to express doubt about what was said. | C ✓ | ✓

    D   to express his impatience. | D |

19 Who did Fotheringay really want to convince?

    A   The landlord, Cox. | A |

    B   Miss Maybridge. | B |

    C   The cyclist. | C |

    D   Mr Beamish. | D ✓ | ✓

20 Of those watching, the one who neither agreed nor disagreed with Fotheringay's definition of a miracle was

    A   the landlord. | A ✓ | ✓

    B   the cyclist. | B |

    C   Mr Beamish. | C |

    D   the landlady. | D |

21 Fotheringay said 'Hullo!'

    A   in answer to Beamish's greeting.

    B   just to be polite.

    C   to greet someone who had just walked in.

    D   because he was so surprised.

A
B
C
D ✓	✓

22 Why did Miss Maybridge scream?

    A   She thought the cyclist was going to attack her.

    B   Fotheringay was staring at her with an evil look.

    C   A duck suddenly leaped onto the bar from somewhere.

    D   She saw the lamp hanging upside-down in the air.

A
B
C
D ✓	✓

PAPER 5 INTERVIEW (Time: approx. 15 minutes)

1 *Study this photo carefully. Then answer the questions below and be prepared to discuss one or more of the related topics.*

Questions

1 Where was this photo probably taken?
2 What has just happened, or what do you think is about to happen?
3 What do you think might have caused this situation?
4 Will the race be stopped? Why?/Why not?
5 Would *you* like to drive in a Grand Prix race? Why?/Why not?

Topics

Dangerous sports
Sport and advertising
The attraction of different sports
Your own hobbies and interests

Note: In the Cambridge Proficiency Exam Interview, you will only see the photo: you will not see the questions. An examiner will ask you them.

2   *Study this passage for a few moments. Then say who you think might have said it (to whom), where and when. Finally read it aloud.*

> I would have thought that the most sensible solution to your particular problem would be for you to have a water softener of some kind installed as soon as possible. Apart from the fact that your washing water is very hard, you must have to clean the fur out of your kettle quite often. And I hate to think what the inside of your water tank, the boiler and the hot water pipes must look like. If the system hasn't been cleaned since it was installed ten years ago, I'm amazed any water is getting through at all! They must be almost totally furred up!

3   *Study the following topics and notes. You should be prepared to speak on any of the topics from your own point of view or from one of the points of view given. When you have been told what your task is, make brief notes before the discussion.*

a)   Topic: The increase in crime – what is the answer?

A social worker who believes that 'community service' is the answer, not prison.
A parent who feels that schools should give more 'moral education'.
A policeman who thinks that deterrents to crime are not hard enough.
A prison warden who believes that too many prisons are too crowded because many (e.g. mentally sick) should not be there.
A religious leader who feels that the Church is losing its influence over people's lives.

b)   Topic: Animal Rights – have they got any?

A scientist who uses animals in experiments to find or test new drugs.
A vegetarian who believes that humans have 'no right' to eat animal flesh.
A member of an animal protection society (e.g. the Royal Society for the Prevention of Cruelty to Animals – RSPCA for short) who is disgusted at 'man's inhumanity to animals'.
A person who believes that man is superior to all other creatures and can use them as he wants to.
A zoologist who is concerned about the increase in the number of endangered species and the effect on the world's ecology.

4   *Read the news report below and then tell your partners about it in your own words. Tell them also what you think about the implications of the article and ask them for their comments.*

Woman Protestor Jailed

Hightown, 20th June

A 45-year-old mother of three was convicted today of breaking into the nuclear power plant at Long Down and daubing an anti-nuclear slogan on the wall of the main administration building. The 'NO NO NO TO NUCLEAR POWER' slogan was painted in 2-foot-high red letters.

A security officer from the plant stated that the accused had got in through the security fence during the night and taken a ladder from a storeroom in order to paint the wall of the building.

In her defence the accused said: 'If people don't protest and take action now, our children will have no future.'

A spokesman from Long Down declared that security at the plant will now be intensified.

The accused, Mrs Jane Seegram, was given a 14-day prison sentence by the Court.

LISTENING COMPREHENSION TEXTS

The following pages contain transcripts of all the Listening Comprehension texts used in Presentation and other phases of Units in the Coursebook, excluding the texts used in Listening Comprehension Tests (Units 4, 9 and 14, and Paper 4 of the Practice Exam), transcripts of which are to be found in the Teacher's Guide only.

Unit 2

TUTOR: Unit 2. Generations.
Look at page 16, Exercise 2.
You're going to hear a radio interview with a sociologist. Listen to find out his general views about the family today and about substitute parents. Ready?

INTERVIEWER: We seem to be hearing more and more nowadays about the 'breakup of the family', that 'parents aren't as good as they used to be' or that 'the lack of good old-fashioned family life is one of the main causes of the rise in juvenile crime'. To look at the family and the role of parents in this day and age, we've invited to the studio Dr Neil, a well-known sociologist. Dr Neil, are parents 'worse' than they used to be? *Is* the family breaking up?

DR NEIL: Well, let's remember first of all that people have been saying for years that 'the family and family life's going to the dogs'. But in spite of that, I think family life *is* different now, and noticeably different.

INTERVIEWER: In what way?

DR NEIL: In a number of ways. You see, in addition to a substantial increase in divorce in many countries, um fewer people are getting re-married.

INTERVIEWER: So you're saying that there are now more one-parent or single-parent families.

DR NEIL: Oh, yes, most definitely. Far more than there ever used to be. But not only are there more one-parent families, but families in general seem to be smaller. And the reason(s) for that are numerous.

INTERVIEWER: Nevertheless, there must also be other differences between family life now and that of, say, thirty or forty years ago. What about families in which both parents go out to work?

DR NEIL: Yes. 'Dual career' families, as we call them, are much more common. And what's more, parents who both want to continue with their careers often do so when their children are still very young indeed.

INTERVIEWER: Yes, we receive a lot of letters from people who disapprove of mothers going on with full-time careers while their children are still toddlers. But besides these differences, I know that you have recently highlighted in some of your research yet another way in which the family unit is different now.

DR NEIL: Yes, the 'substitute parent'. More and more parents, certainly in the United States and in England and other European countries, are paying more people to look after their children. They're paying for substitutes, if you like.

INTERVIEWER: You mean, like baby-sitters, play groups and so on.

DR NEIL: Yes, but there are other substitutes as well of course. Teachers, youth club leaders, . . .

INTERVIEWER: And television, in its own way?

DR NEIL: Most definitely.

INTERVIEWER: Let's go back to teachers for the moment. Um primary school teachers have always really had er er a substitute parent role, haven't they? Whereas the teachers of older children teach reading, writing and academic subjects, the primary school teacher has always reinforced what the parents are doing – helping children to acquire good habits and so on. As well as perhaps to start them reading and writing.

DR NEIL: Yes, and sometimes the situation has created confusion.

INTERVIEWER: Oh, you mean, because of different 'messages' that children might be getting from parents and teachers.

DR NEIL: Yes.

INTERVIEWER: There are people now of course who think that, because of more parents going out to work, teachers of older children should take on – or at least be aware of the fact that they are parent substitutes?

DR NEIL: Yes, there are people who think that. But it's very difficult because of the amount of time teachers have in which to teach what they have to teach.

INTERVIEWER: Can we go back for a moment to smaller families, which we mentioned earlier? Are there perhaps any noticeable effects of smaller families?

DR NEIL: Yes, the main thing, I think, is that there's less mixing of ages. It's said, for example, that girls learn to be parents by being involved with younger children . . .

INTERVIEWER: And fewer children are mixing with younger children.

DR NEIL: Yes.

INTERVIEWER: But that's not of primary importance, I would have thought. It seems to me that what a child really needs is a loving environment – and you can't get that when TV is the substitute parent, for instance.

DR NEIL: Yes, television worries me. A child needs basic trust and love and a commitment from a human being. All the other substitutes – baby-sitters, play group and primary school teachers, youth club leaders and so on – fine.

In their own way, and to varying degrees, they can all offer a child love and understanding. But not the square screen!

INTERVIEWER: In other words, you don't mind other *people* looking after your children –

DR NEIL: No.

INTERVIEWER: – but you object to television taking over your role.

DR NEIL: Yes. What I'm objecting to is the economic situation which forces many parents to go out to work and does not allow them to spend as much time with their children as I think parents ought to.

INTERVIEWER: Well, perhaps before we pursue this further, we should open our phone-lines for listeners to ring in . . . . . .

TUTOR: Now rewind the tape and look at Exercise 3. Listen again and make notes.
And that's the end of Unit 2.

Unit 3

TUTOR: Unit 3. Mysteries and Theories
Look at page 21, Listening. You're going to hear a radio interview with an author. Listen and make notes on the facts of what happened and on the different theories. Ready?

INTERVIEWER: That record was for Susan in Oxford. And now for our 'Meet the Authors' spot this week, and I'm pleased to have with me the author of a new book on mysteries of the world, Mark Tayler. Good evening, Mark.

MARK: Good evening.

INTERVIEWER: Now, lots of people nowadays seem to be interested in the mysterious, the weird and wonderful, and so on . . .

MARK: Yes, they are, and that's obviously one reason why I wrote the book.

INTERVIEWER: Well, I've read the book and it really is quite fascinating. It's full of accounts of strange happenings, but you've rethought many of the theories that have been put forward to date, haven't you?

MARK: Yes, I have. And I suppose I have been over-critical of some of the explanations that have been suggested to account for certain happenings and events in the past. But there is one that's so extraordinary that all I've been able to do is re-state what others have said before.

INTERVIEWER: And which is that? The Curse of the Pharaohs?

MARK: No, I'm talking about the mystery of the 'Mary Celeste'.

INTERVIEWER: Ah. Well, could you tell us some of the theories about what might have happened on that ship?

MARK: Yes, of course. But in view of the time at my disposal I'll have to over-simplify things a little. Briefly the facts are these: In October, 1872, the 'Mary Celeste', she was a cargo sailing ship, set sail from New York for Genoa under Captain Briggs. On board were his wife and 2-year-old daughter, and 8 crew. A month later, the ship was found sailing around erratically in the Azores by a Captain Moorhouse who was sailing his ship to Gibraltar. The 'Mary Celeste' was abandoned, deserted. The one lifeboat was missing, as were the navigation instruments and the ship's papers, and there was some water in the hold, but all the cargo was intact. Everything seemed to have been left behind as if everyone had left in a great hurry.

INTERVIEWER: Strange, isn't it?

MARK: Yes, you see the real mystery is: why was the ship completely abandoned, and if the crew escaped in the lifeboat, why didn't they take provisions with them?

INTERVIEWER: Hmm.

MARK: Well, there are almost dozens of theories, but they all kind of fall under three headings: firstly, illness or insanity; secondly, violence or piracy, which was not unknown then; and thirdly, crisis at sea.

INTERVIEWER: Well, what about illness or insanity as a possible explanation?

MARK: Well, it's been suggested that everyone on board was poisoned somehow, either by fungus in the bread, or a poisonous gas either from fungus in the ship's timbers or even from the sea. At any rate, the suggestion is that they were all driven mad and jumped overboard or tried to escape in the lifeboat. Like all the explanations, it's possible, I suppose.

INTERVIEWER: But you also mentioned insanity.

MARK: Yes, it has been suggested that the captain, who was fervently religious, by the way, basically went mad and murdered everyone and then threw himself into the sea. Well, I don't think that's very plausible, but there's nothing to disprove it.

INTERVIEWER: How about the violence or piracy theories?

MARK: One of the 'violence' theories suggests that the crew drank some of the alcohol which the ship was carrying, then murdered the captain and his family, then, when they realised what they'd done, they dropped the bodies overboard and abandoned the ship in the lifeboat. It's a theory.

INTERVIEWER: You sound doubtful about all the theories you've given us to date. What about the 'crisis at sea' solution?

MARK: Well, this makes much better sense, in my view, but the whole problem with the mystery is you can't prove or disprove anything completely. I personally think there was a crisis of some kind. One suggestion is that one of the sailors went down into the hold and found water in it. Thinking that the ship was sinking, or was going to sink, he shouted the alarm and everyone rushed for the lifeboat and abandoned ship as quickly as possible. There are a number of objections to that theory as there are with all the others.

INTERVIEWER: It's a fascinating mystery, Mark, but I'm afraid that's all we've time for. So I'd just like to thank you for coming to the studio today and to recommend . . .

TUTOR:	If you wish to listen to the interview again, rewind the tape. And that's the end of Unit 3.

Unit 4

TUTOR:	Now look at page 24, Exercise 1b. You're going to hear extracts from a newspaper article read by people with different 'non-standard' English accents. As you listen, write in the number of the speaker against the accent. Ready?
	One.
SCOTTISH:	During the past few years, town and city planners in Britain have been drawing up plans for the city environment of the future. Their main concern is to eliminate weak spots, hiding places and temptation in order to reduce the amount of vandalism, mugging and burglary.
TUTOR:	Two.
AUSTRALIAN:	Criminals need hiding places, such as tall hedges, fences, doorways, and so on, so the city environment of the future will have wide open spaces. And paths and other pedestrian areas will be lit at night with streetlights that should be vandal-proof.
TUTOR:	Three.
WELSH:	Security will be one of the prime considerations in the design of buildings. Visitors to blocks of flats or private houses will be checked either by caretakers or by remote control television monitors.
TUTOR:	Four.
AMERICAN:	All of these proposed measures, and there are many more, will be put together under three new British Standards – one for dwellings, another for commercial and industrial premises, and a third for public places.
TUTOR:	Five.
CARIBBEAN:	Work began back in 1982 with the first meeting of a new British Standards Institute committee. Represented were members of the police, the security and insurance industries, local authorities, surveyors, architects, fire officers, and many more.
TUTOR:	Six.
SOUTH AFRICAN:	The aim of this new BSI committee is to produce what is in effect a comprehensive security blueprint. In one document, it hopes to reproduce all the available information on vandal-proof street furniture, locks, and security doors and windows.
TUTOR:	Seven.
IRISH:	In the future, every citizen will not be regarded as innocent and law-abiding. Instead, in order to lead a trouble-free daily life, he will have to be prepared to prove his innocence. In an attempt to deter terrorist bombers, the citizens . . .
TUTOR:	Now rewind the tape, listen again and check your answers with a partner and the class.

TUTOR:	Now look at page 24, Exercise 2b. You're going to hear someone talking about the rise in crime. As you listen, fill in the missing information in the four boxes. Don't worry if you miss something the first time.
WOMAN:	Sad though it is, we have to admit that crime is on the increase, especially in large cities like London. Not only have muggings, burglaries and car thefts become more and more common, but *all* crimes apparently. These are the frightening figures for *all crimes* committed in London: there were 354,445 recorded crimes in London back in 1972. By 1982, only ten years later, that figure had more than doubled to a staggering 688,179. 688,179! But the most frightening of all is the almost unbelievable, and very worrying rise in *armed robbery* over the same period, from 380 recorded cases in 1972 to not far off 2,000 in 1982. To be precise, there were 1,772 recorded cases of armed robbery in London in that year. That's 400 per cent more than were committed ten years before!
TUTOR:	Now rewind the tape, listen again and check your answers with a partner and the class.
TUTOR:	Look at page 25, Exercise 2. You're going to hear two people being interviewed in the street as part of an opinion poll to discover the attitudes of the general public to certain social problems. As you listen, fill in the chart as if you were the interviewer. Mark 'M' for the man's opinions, and 'W' for the woman's. Ready?
INTERVIEWER:	Now the next question.
MAN:	Yes.
INTERVIEWER:	I'm going to read out a list of crimes and for each one I'd like you to tell me which of the sentences on the card you feel should represent the *maximum* sentence imposed by the courts.
MAN:	Hmm . . . hmm . . .
INTERVIEWER:	Bigamy.
MAN:	Oh . . . don't know, really.
INTERVIEWER:	Blackmail?
MAN:	Well, that's becoming a lot more common. Certainly a sentence of some kind . . . imprisonment . . . Oh, seven or eight years.
INTERVIEWER:	Mm. Possession of drugs?
MAN:	About the same. Perhaps a little longer. Say ten years. I must say I'm absolutely disgusted at the way people like that spread . . . um . . .
INTERVIEWER:	Yes. Hijacking?
MAN:	Hijacking? Oh, about 15 years in prison. Definitely.
INTERVIEWER:	Kidnapping?
MAN:	The same. 15 years.
INTERVIEWER:	Murder.
MAN:	You couldn't have a list of crimes without murder, could you? Life. Life imprisonment. And by that, I mean for the rest of the murderer's life. Not let out for good behaviour after ten years.

INTERVIEWER:	Armed robbery?
MAN:	Ten years.
INTERVIEWER:	Theft, including shoplifting.
MAN:	Oh, including shoplifting. That's difficult. I would have said 'no sentence' for shoplifting: at least, not a prison sentence. I don't know. Perhaps a year or so.
INTERVIEWER:	Rape and other sexual offences.
MAN:	Life. No doubt about it. Life in prison. I think a lot of people are deeply disturbed at the way these particular crimes have increased in recent years.
INTERVIEWER:	And lastly, mugging.
MAN:	Well, I'd put that on a level with armed robbery and say at least ten years. No, more: at least 12 years.
INTERVIEWER:	Thank you. Now there's just one more question . . . . . .
TUTOR:	Now listen to the second person being interviewed.
INTERVIEWER:	. . . which of the sentences on the card you feel should represent the *maximum* sentence imposed by the courts. The first is bigamy.
WOMAN:	Bigamy? Ah . . . well, I think it's an utterly despicable thing for a man to do in Britain, marry two wives. It's different in other societies, isn't it? Oh, I don't know. 5 years in prison, perhaps.
INTERVIEWER:	Blackmail.
WOMAN:	Fifteen years, I'd say.
INTERVIEWER:	And possession of drugs?
WOMAN:	The same. About 15 years.
INTERVIEWER:	Hijacking?
WOMAN:	I find the rise in hijackings round the world absolutely appalling. And I think the only way to stop it is to impose the maximum prison sentence you can: life.
INTERVIEWER:	Kidnapping.
WOMAN:	It's the same story, although it's obviously a great deal worse in some countries than in others. Nevertheless, in my opinion, life imprisonment is the only answer. The sentence should at least act as a deterrent.
INTERVIEWER:	And murder?
WOMAN:	The death penalty.
INTERVIEWER:	Armed robbery.
WOMAN:	About fifteen or twenty years in prison, I think. After all, it's the one crime which has almost certainly risen – sorry, increased more than any other in the past few years. Perhaps longer terms of imprisonment, or at least the threat of longer sentences, might help reduce the number of armed robberies.
INTERVIEWER:	Theft, including shoplifting.
WOMAN:	I would say something like six, seven, eight years, depending on the crime, the amount stolen and so on. Even shoplifters should receive much longer sentences than they do. I'm absolutely amazed at the way shoplifters – thieves – are often let off scot-free. At least that's what I think.
INTERVIEWER:	Rape and sexual assault.
WOMAN:	Again the frequency of these kind of crimes is frightening. But I really don't know what the answer is, and I honestly don't know what sentence a rapist should be given in court. I wish I did, but I just don't know.

INTERVIEWER:	And finally, mugging.
WOMAN:	Mugging. There was a case in the papers the other day where an old lady in her 80s was mugged by two youths and badly beaten – just for a few pounds. They've got to give muggers life. Definitely, life.
INTERVIEWER:	Thank you. Now there's just one more question . . .
TUTOR:	If you wish to listen to the interviews again, rewind the tape.
TUTOR:	Look at page 27, Vocabulary. You're going to hear a number of people saying things and expressing different emotions. As you listen, decide what feeling the speaker is expressing and write down a phrase to describe it e.g. 'deeply offended', 'absolutely determined', etc. There'll be a short pause after each one to allow you to write down what you think. Ready?
	One.
AMERICAN:	You say you've passed the exam? That's incredible! You never thought you'd pass, did you?'
TUTOR:	Two.
SCOT:	Oh no. Oh, that's really bad news. He'll be so upset. I really thought he stood a good chance. That's awful.
TUTOR:	Three.
STANDARD:	Oh, for goodness' sake! Can't you get anything right?!
TUTOR:	Four.
WELSH:	Ugh! You're not going to *eat* that, are you?! It looks *dreadful*! Ugh!
TUTOR:	Five.
S. AFRICAN:	Phew! After all that exercise, I'm worn out!
TUTOR:	Six.
STANDARD:	How could he have said that to me? I just don't understand. How could he have treated me like that?
TUTOR:	Seven.
AUSTRALIAN:	That was very funny. Really – very, very funny!
TUTOR:	Eight.
IRISH:	I'm going to finish putting this table together if it's the last thing I do!
TUTOR:	Nine.
CARIBBEAN:	I think that must be the most moving film I've seen for a very long time. It was done so beautifully.
TUTOR:	Ten.
STANDARD:	I just don't feel like it, that's all. I just can't be bothered . . . I don't know . . . I just don't . . . I just don't want to do anything.
TUTOR:	If you wish to listen again, rewind the tape.

Unit 5

| TUTOR: | Unit 5. Consumer Society. Look at page 33, Listening. |

Listen to this advertisement. It's the kind of thing you might hear on a commercial radio station.

1ST VOICE: Calling all harassed businessmen! Do you have to run off copies of reports, letters, leaflets, accounts at short notice? Do you need a quick copy of that letter and can't wait for someone to retype it for you? If so, then you're the sort of person who needs the new KOPI-ALL photocopier!
Being the busy person you are, you'll wonder how you've ever managed without a photocopier like this. And having once used the KOPI-ALL machine, you'll never need to be harassed again.

MR JAMES: KOPI-ALL's a wonderful machine. I can certainly recommend it. We've only had ours for a month, but already business is picking up and my secretaries wonder how they ever managed before. It's fast, it photocopies four different sizes of paper, it reduces and expands drawings or photos - and what's most amazing, it'll copy colour.

1ST VOICE: So you see. No sooner had Mr James had a KOPI-ALL installed than his business showed signs of improvement.

2ND VOICE: Remember. KOPI-ALL will save you time and money – and worry. And not only does it make photocopies – any other photocopier will do that – but it photocopies in different sizes, and in black and white or colour.

1ST VOICE: And the cost? Incredible as it is, a KOPI-ALL could be yours for only £25 a month, with free installation and servicing. This offer lasts for a month from today. So the longer you wait, the more you could regret it.

2ND VOICE: KOPI-ALL. It copies everything – perfectly.

TUTOR: If you wish to listen to the advertisement again, rewind the tape.

Unit 7

TUTOR: Unit 7. The Energy Debate.
Look at page 48. You're going to hear part of a serious radio programme in which two politicians discuss nuclear energy. Listen to it once and say what position each speaker holds on the subject. Ready?

MAN: The way to reduce imports is not to bring the bullock back into farming, but to build nuclear power stations. That way, there's no dependence on any foreign power for energy supplies.

WOMAN: I'm afraid that's far from being the case. You may not have to import the energy, but you do have to import uranium and also all the technology required to build and run a nuclear power plant.

MAN: That may be, but once a nuclear plant has been built, you don't need to go on importing technology, and actual running costs are low so we'd have more of the taxpayers' money available to finance, well, the social services, for example.

WOMAN: I think once again you're overlooking a very important point: the running costs of a nuclear plant may well be relatively low, but the initial capital

expenditure is astronomical! It involves sums that our present-day economy certainly couldn't entertain, so the only way we could build a nuclear plant would be by international borrowing, and then how could we talk of being independent of any foreign power? No, to my mind, nuclear power means two things only – dependence and danger . . .

MAN: That, for me, is an example of muddled thinking. For so many people the main association of the word 'nuclear' is, well – understandably, bombs and war. And people bring all these fears to any discussion of nuclear power, when in fact all nuclear plants have to conform to the strictest safety and security measures, and they have an excellent record of accident-free operation.

WOMAN: Perhaps they have, but the same can't be said for the disposal of nuclear waste, a factor you seem not to be considering . . .

MAN: As you well know, the utmost care is taken to dispose of waste, and once again our record has been a good one, which I'm afraid can't be said of other energy industries. We all know only too well how oil has polluted our seas and beaches and killed off marine life. We've watched coal mines scar our landscape and pollute our air, not to mention the diseases miners run the risk of catching. Of course, solar energy is a safe clean source of energy, but we're all well aware of how limited its applications are. In today's day and age I see little alternative to meeting our energy needs outside nuclear power.

WOMAN: Once again you seem to be closing your eyes to a vital issue: conservation. To my mind, conservation is the one thing that all those in favour of nuclear energy . . . . . .

TUTOR: Now rewind the tape, listen to the discussion again and note the arguments expressed for and against nuclear energy.
And that's the end of Unit 7.

Unit 9

TUTOR: Unit 9. Personal Experiences.
Look at page 60, Exercise 1.
Listen to this short anecdote, and then answer the questions. Ready?

MAN: I was at one of those 'Music and Words' evenings at our local hall. You know, an evening of songs and poetry readings by local amateurs. There was a woman on the stage reading a poem. She had such a rasping voice that I turned to the man sitting next to me and, in a whisper, commented on it. He looked at me rather frostily and whispered back: 'That's my wife.' Not knowing quite what to do, and beginning to blush, I muttered: 'Oh, I didn't really mean her voice: I meant the poem she's reading.' He looked at me again and hissed: 'I wrote it.'
I slumped down in my seat and hid my face. It was as near as I could get to disappearing through a hole in the floor!

TUTOR: Look at page 61, Exercise 3. Listen and answer the multiple-choice questions. Ready?

WOMAN: The situation I'm going to tell you about is one in which I could have dropped tons of bricks – and probably did!

A few years ago – I'd been a reporter on a national magazine for about two years, I think – I was invited along to one of those big parties in aid of charity. You know the kind – the sort of party where everyone is a celebrity, a 'famous name'. Well, I found myself in conversation with a man who'd been introduced to me, but I hadn't listened to the name. His face was familiar, but the name just wouldn't come. It was exasperating.

Anyway, we chatted amicably for twenty minutes or so. He seemed to know my name, asked how things were on the magazine, (and) even asked after my family; although how he knew about my work and my family, I just couldn't think. In return, as you do in polite conversation, I asked him what he did, how his career was going, how his wife was, and so on. All his answers were pretty vague, I thought. I was intrigued to find that he travelled a lot, and asked him if he took his wife when he travelled. On being told that they often travelled separately in Britain, but usually travelled abroad together, 'as I must know', I began to feel somewhat baffled, and also felt that I should know who he was. With a somewhat uncomfortable feeling, and a politely whispered 'It was very nice to meet you', I managed to extricate myself and made for the Ladies' Room.

It wasn't until after I reached the haven of the Ladies' Room and closed the door on the buzz of the party that the realisation dawned – I'd been speaking to the Duke of Edinburgh, and had actually asked him his career was going! and how his wife (the Queen!) was! And of course he knew me! I had had the great fortune to interview him briefly for an article in my first year on the magazine. I could have died! – I didn't, of course. Instead, I collected my coat and slunk away, extremely flushed.

TUTOR: To listen to the anecdote again, rewind the tape.

TUTOR: Look at page 61, Exercise 5. You're going to hear an extract from a radio programme about disasters and how people cope with them. Listen and answer the multiple-choice questions.

NARRATOR: . . . so disasters can in fact be major, or quite minor events in people's lives. It all depends how the people involved regard them.

For six years John Noakes had planned the voyage that would take him, his wife Vicky and their 14-metre boat halfway round the world, down into the Caribbean and the paradise island of Antigua.

In September '82, ten weeks out to sea, a freak storm blew up, and in a force 9 gale the Noakes' boat was shattered by a 20-metre wave that left the couple adrift for a day and a half off Spain.

The storm claimed 22 lives, but John and Vicky survived to be picked up by a passing tanker.

Back in England, John found it very difficult to steer clear of thoughts of sun-soaked West Indian islands.

'It's so depressing,' he moaned, staring out of his office window. 'But we're going back to sea. The first thing my wife said after the tanker had picked us up was, "We'll get the boat repaired, and set off again". I thought "Good grief – what have I married?".'

Asked about the experience of being shipwrecked, John said: 'I kept thinking that if we'd set off two days later, we would have missed the storm. But at the time, no one expected a hurricane-force gale. We were just told to anticipate strong winds.

'Shortly before we were knocked down, I went up on deck and saw the biggest wave I'd ever seen. It was moving in slow motion and as a piece of power it was really quite beautiful. There was no time to be terrified. I just got back down below, and it was all over in a flash. I think we were lifted to the crest of the wave, then ran out of water, so the boat toppled down, with the wave crashing over us.'

TUTOR: To listen to the extract again, rewind the tape.

TUTOR: Look at page 62 and listen. You're going to hear a radio news item. Ready?

NEWSREADER: The time is 9 o'clock and here is the news.

Figures published today indicate for the first time in six months that there has been a noticeable improvement in the country's economic situation. Speaking at the headquarters of the National Economic Council, a spokesman declared that the figures were very good news indeed for industry and for the rest of the country. When asked about the possibility of lower bank rates to help borrowing, however, he replied that it was far too early to tell, although he doubted whether the figures would force any such changes just yet. The spokesman added that the Council would be making a fuller statement when the figures had been analysed in detail.

TUTOR: If you wish to hear the news item again, rewind the tape.

TUTOR: Look at page 62, Exercise 2. You're going to hear three interviews. Listen and report what was said.

The first is with Cliff Priestley at his London flat.

INTERVIEWER: Cliff, you're said to be one of the richest pop stars in the country, and there are rumours that you're leaving for the USA. Can you comment on that?

CLIFF: No, I'm definitely not leaving. And, to be honest, I'm infuriated by accusations like that.

INTERVIEWER: Infuriated?

CLIFF: Yes. Basically, I'm being accused of not wanting to pay taxes, aren't I?

INTERVIEWER: Well, I don't know. But how do you think these rumours started?

CLIFF: I assume someone misunderstood the announcement about my forthcoming tour of the States. I'm very patriotic, and although obviously I pay a lot of Income Tax, I certainly don't want to leave this country to go and live in the States.

INTERVIEWER: So what do you think of certain other artists and groups in the pop business who have left for the States? To live there permanently, I mean.

CLIFF: I'm concerned that people who've had some success feel obliged to leave for tax reasons – but I don't agree with them.

TUTOR: The second interview is with a spokesman for British Rail about a goods train which was derailed earlier today.

INTERVIEWER: Can you give us any more information about the derailment?

SPOKESMAN: No, I'm sorry I can't. We're mystified. It's the third on this stretch of line in the past month.

INTERVIEWER: So is there any connection between this and the previous two, do you think?

SPOKESMAN: It's possible. There could be. But we've found no evidence as yet to prove any connection.

INTERVIEWER: I presume you know the causes of the previous two?

SPOKESMAN: Yes. On the previous two occasions, the derailments were caused by large stones which had been thrown onto the line from a bridge. There's no evidence that this happened here.

INTERVIEWER: Were there any casualties?

SPOKESMAN: No, no one was hurt. And the line was only closed for twelve hours. It's open again now.

TUTOR: And the third interview is with a policeman at the scene of an accident.

INTERVIEWER: Sergeant, I wonder if you can tell me what happened?

POLICE SERGEANT: Well, we're not quite sure at the moment. All we know is that three cars collided at the traffic lights here, and that all the occupants of the three cars have been taken to hospital for treatment.

INTERVIEWER: Are any of them badly injured?

SERGEANT: No, none. I believe they're all badly shaken.

INTERVIEWER: Have you taken any statements yet?

SERGEANT: No, not yet. We shall be interviewing them later. In the meantime, we want to get the road cleared.

INTERVIEWER: And you've no way of knowing how the accident happened?

SERGEANT: No. Nothing certain. The lights were reported to be faulty earlier today, so they may have stopped working. In which case, as you'll know, it's every man for himself. All three may have thought it was safe to cross. But at the moment we just don't know.

TUTOR: Now rewind the tape, listen to the three interviews again and extract the main points from each in order to write news items.

Unit 14

TUTOR: Unit 14. Leisure and Health. Look at page 100, Exercise 3.
Look at the questionnaire and listen. You'll hear a man and woman being interviewed in the street. As you listen to their answers, fill in the questionnaire with 'M' for the man's answers, 'W' for the woman's answers. Ready?

INTERVIEWER: Excuse me.

MAN: Yes.

INTERVIEWER: I wonder if you and your wife would answer a questionnaire for an opinion poll that we're doing on pastimes and leisure?

MAN: Yes, of course.

WOMAN: Well, I don't know, George. It's getting very late, and, you know, . . .

INTERVIEWER: Well, if you'd rather not . . .

MAN: No, no it's fine. You go ahead.

INTERVIEWER: Well, then, do you agree or disagree with this statement? 'I don't have enough leisure time.'

MAN: Oh, disagree, definitely. I have plenty of leisure time.

WOMAN: Well, I don't. I never seem to have time for anything I want to do. . .

MAN: Yes, dear. Let's get on with it, can we?

INTERVIEWER: Now, can you tell me how often you do the following things: Every day? Once or twice a week? Once a month? Very rarely? Or never? How often do you read a book?

MAN: Every day.

WOMAN: How often do I ever have time to read a book? Once in a blue moon, if I'm lucky.

INTERVIEWER: Er, yes. How often do you watch television or listen to the radio?

WOMAN: Oh, we watch television every evening, don't we, George? We love it!

MAN: It's all right, if you like everything they put on. But radio. Now that's different. I still think it's great and I listen to it every day in the car.

WOMAN: I think I only ever turn the radio on once or twice a week.

INTERVIEWER: How about indoor games? Do you ever play cards, or Monopoly, or Scrabble . . . ?

WOMAN: Oh, very rarely.

MAN: But I play cards once a month, down at the club.

INTERVIEWER: Video games?

WOMAN:	No, never. We haven't got a video, have we, George?
MAN:	No. But I'd like to buy one. I think they're excellent!
INTERVIEWER:	Do either of you play any outdoor games? You know, tennis? Golf?
WOMAN:	No, nothing like that, never.
INTERVIEWER:	And you, sir?
MAN:	No, I don't play tennis, or anything. But I try to go swimming once a week, and we both go for a long walk about once a month, I suppose.
WOMAN:	Good heavens! I never thought I'd hear him say it! George! – we go for a long walk just occasionally. Certainly not once a month!
MAN:	Yes, she's right, of course. About the walking I mean. But I *do* go swimming once a week.
INTERVIEWER:	Now, how often do you do these things? Go to . . .
MAN:	Ouch! I think I've just been stung on my neck!
WOMAN:	Oh, no! Let me have a look.
MAN:	Pheew!
WOMAN:	Yes, there is a sting there. I can see it. A wasp's sting, I think. Just hold on and I'll try and get it out. It won't hurt. Ah, there it is!
MAN:	Phew! I thought you said it wouldn't hurt!
WOMAN:	Well . . . I think we'd better get to the nearest chemist and get something for that. Will you excuse us?
INTERVIEWER:	Well, could we quickly finish the questions perhaps?
MAN:	Yes, all right, but very quickly.
INTERVIEWER:	Well, as I was saying, how often do you do these things? Go to the cinema?
MAN:	Never.
INTERVIEWER:	Go to the theatre, opera or ballet?
MAN:	Ballet? Yuk! No, never.
WOMAN:	No, never. Any of them.
INTERVIEWER:	Go to a concert?
WOMAN:	Occasionally.
INTERVIEWER:	Go to an art gallery, museum, etc?
MAN:	Oh, about once a month. I enjoy going to museums. Pheew! This is hurting! How many more questions?
INTERVIEWER:	Not many. Now, do either of you play an instrument?
WOMAN:	No.
INTERVIEWER:	Uh-huh. Do either of you sing in a choir?
MAN:	No.
INTERVIEWER:	Do you ever go to the beach or a lake?
WOMAN:	Well, once a year really. We always have a seaside holiday.
INTERVIEWER:	Fine. How about going fishing or hunting?
WOMAN:	No.
MAN:	Oh, I love fishing. I can think of nothing better than sitting on a river bank in the pouring rain . . .
WOMAN:	George! Don't take any notice of him.
INTERVIEWER:	No. Do you go cycling, climbing, or anything?
MAN:	No.
INTERVIEWER:	Do either of you paint?
MAN:	No. And how many more questions?
INTERVIEWER:	Only one or two. Do you attend a club of any kind?

MAN:	Yes, a social club twice a week.
WOMAN:	I go to an antiques club once a month.
INTERVIEWER:	And the last question . . .
MAN:	About time, too!
INTERVIEWER:	Do you help other people? You know, the elderly, the disabled . . .?
WOMAN:	Well, neither of us does at the moment, but I've just put my name down to help at an Old People's Club . . .
MAN:	I didn't know anything about that! You might have *told* me! Anyway, let's get to that chemist's and get something . . .
INTERVIEWER:	Er, thank you very much!
TUTOR:	To listen to the interview again, rewind the tape.
TUTOR:	Look at page 101, Exercise 2. Listen to these brief extracts from the interview with the man and woman again and answer the four multiple-choice questions. Ready?
	One.
WOMAN:	Oh, we watch television every evening, don't we, George? We love it!
MAN:	It's all right, if you like everything they put on. But radio. Now that's different. I still think it's great and I listen to it every day in the car.
TUTOR:	Two.
WOMAN:	Oh, no! Let me have a look.
MAN:	Pheew!
WOMAN:	Yes, there is a sting there. I can see it.
TUTOR:	Three.
INTERVIEWER:	Fine. How about going fishing or hunting?
WOMAN:	No.
MAN:	Oh, I love fishing. I can think of nothing better than sitting on a river bank in the pouring rain . . .
WOMAN:	George!
TUTOR:	Four.
INTERVIEWER:	Do either of you paint?
MAN:	No. And how many more questions?
INTERVIEWER:	Only one or two.
TUTOR:	Now rewind the tape, listen again and check your answers.
TUTOR:	Look at page 102, Exercise 2. You're going to hear two people telling someone else about the article in Exercise 1. Listen to each and say which is using formal and which informal speech. You must give reasons. Ready?
	One.
MAN:	The article by Geoffrey Cannon about exercise I found most illuminating. What was interesting, I think, was not only that he had taken up running as a result of basically being unable to lose weight by dieting, but that he started to investigate the weight loss which seemed to surprise him. As he said, in theory, exercise is not a particularly effective way of losing weight, and yet in practice it most certainly would

141

	seem to be extremely effective. The reason, according to him, is that running, together with certain other types of exercise, increases the metabolic rate and you thus burn more calories.
TUTOR:	Two.
WOMAN:	I read an article the other day that was very interesting. It was by a man who'd dieted for years, but never lost any weight. But then he took up jogging to keep his weight down. And it worked. He found out that as long as he went running regularly, he could eat and drink what he wanted. Then he began to look into why exercise helps you lose weight. Apparently all the dieting experts say it doesn't work. Well, apparently the reason is that your metabolism speeds up when you run, and that's good for you because it burns up more calories.
TUTOR:	Now rewind the tape, listen to them again a little more carefully and pick out some of the features which make one more formal than the other.
TUTOR:	Look at page 103, Exercise 2. You're going to hear people from different professions talking about the boom in the 'Keep-Fit' industry. As you listen, put the number of the speaker against the profession. Ready?
	One.
LAWYER:	I suspect that it's already fairly common practice for people going along to aerobics and keep-fit classes and such like to sign something saying that the organisers will not be liable for damage for permanent injury, etc. But whether such documents are legally binding on either party has yet to be seen. There is already one case going through the courts now of a middle-aged man who enrolled in such a course and suffered a heart attack during the first session. He didn't die, but has been ill since. and he and his wife are claiming against the school . . . . . .
TUTOR:	Two.
SOCIOLOGIST:	What I find so interesting is this sudden surge in the past few years for people um people of all ages, from . . . well, I mean, after school-leaving age . . . from 20 to 80, to keep-fit. More and more people are going jogging, swimming regularly, taking up tennis, and so on. And um nowhere is this more noticeable than in the numbers of mainly women going to keep fit or aerobics classes. Cindy Gilbert's classes, for example, grew from one small class of twelve to a staggering 7,000 participants in

	70-odd halls in and around London. This is a clear example of a major change in society itself, and is worthy of study to try to answer questions like: *Is* society coming to terms with increased leisure time? Or is this perhaps only a strange temporary trend?
TUTOR:	Three.
BUSINESSMAN:	One or two of our leading products were certainly in decline, and we were in danger of having to cut back our staff, until there was this new wave of interest in sport and keep-fit. The special gear, kit and clothes we now produce for this market has meant that we have actually increased production and have taken on more staff than we had before. At the moment there is a boom in equipment for the keep-fit movement, and we can hardly keep up with demand. We just hope it continues . . .
TUTOR:	Four.
A DOCTOR:	I am not myself an advocate of dieting. What I recommend to patients often is a change in their way of life, so that they try to get more exercise and balance that with a good varied diet – plenty of vegetables, roughage, fruit and so on. Cut right down on alcohol and try to stop smoking, if they smoke. Of course, some then come back to me with pulled muscles, sprained ankles and the like, but er these are simple things to deal with . . .
TUTOR:	Five.
ARTS COUNSELLOR:	While we're talking about a renewed interest in keep-fit and aerobics, we mustn't forget too there's also been a rise in the number of young people taking up gymnastics quite seriously. And this must soon begin to be reflected in a renewed interest in ballet. At least, I hope it will. Obviously, my own concern is with ballet, opera and music, but keep-fit, aerobics, gymnastics and ballet all have something in common.
TUTOR:	Six.
TOWN PLANNER:	Not so many years ago, a person in my position would have been more concerned with roads, parks, the development of housing estates and so on, but we are now having to think a great deal more about amenities – the provision of sports complexes, landscaping, and so on. My predecessors made some terrible mistakes, which I hope we have learned from now . . .
TUTOR:	Page 103, Exercise 3. Now rewind the tape, listen again and note down words and expressions which the speakers use in connection with their professions.

Acknowledgements

We are grateful to the following for permission to reproduce copyright material:

Century Publishing Co Ltd for an extract from the article 'Why Exercise Makes You Slim' from *Dieting Makes You Fat* (1983) by Geoffrey Cannon & Hetty Einzig; author's agents and Miss D.E. Collins for an extract from the short story 'The Blue Cross' from *The Innocence of Father Brown* by G.K. Chesterton; Collins Publishers for extracts from *The Stationary Ark* by Gerald Durrell (Fontana Paperbacks 1977); Consumers' Association for the adapted article 'Compact Disc' *Which?* magazine Aug 1983; Council of Europe for an extract from the article 'More damage in 20 years than in 24 centuries' by Clino Ferrucci page XVI *Forum* March 1979 and the adapted article 'Treasure Hunting' by Alain Weil pages XV–XVI *Forum* Jan 1981; Granada Publishing Ltd and Alfred A. Knopf Inc for an extract from *2010: Odyssey Two* by Arthur C. Clarke © 1982 by SEREMDIB BV; Granada Publishing Ltd and Alfred A. Knopf Inc for an extract from *The Four Gated City* by Doris © Doris Lessing 1969; Guardian Newspapers Ltd for extracts from the articles 'The New Generation on Skid Row' by W.J. Weatherby *The Guardian* 24.7.83 and 'When the graduate goes home' by Debra Isaacs *The Guardian* 21.8.83; the author Roger Guttridge for an extract from his book *Dorset Smugglers* (1884, Doreset Publishing Co); the author's agents for an extract from *An Alien Agony* by Harry Harrison © Harry Harrison 1962; William Heinemann Ltd and Little, Brown & Co in association with the Atlantic Monthly Press for an extract from *Dear Me* by Peter Ustinov copyright © 1977 by Pavor, S.A; The Hogarth Press for extracts from *Cider With Rosie* by Laurie Lee; Hutchinson Publishing Group Ltd for an adapted extract from *1985* by Anthony Burgess; Institution of Professional Civil Servants for an extract from the article 'April Pension plea' p. 16 *IPCS Bulletin* 11/83 Sept; Michael Joseph Ltd for an extract from *What The Censor Saw* by John Trevelyan; London Express News & Feature Services for the article 'Crashing into Campden Town from the crest of a wave' by David James Smith *TV Times* 17–23rd Sep 1983, the adapted articles 'Burglar' by Martin Leighton *Sunday Express Magazine* 17.7.83 and 'First Fiddle' by Amanda Warren *Sunday Express Magazine* 2.10.83; the author's agents for an adapted extract from *Facing Death* by Brian Magee (pub Wm Kimber); Market & Opinion Research International for a question and a table from page 1 *Attitudes of the General Public*, Monthly Poll for The Daily Express July 1978; The New York Times for the article 'Insects eat mummies in Peru's museums' by Edward Schumacher *The New York Times* 30.8.83 Copyright © 1983 by The New York Times Co; The Observer News Service for the article 'A Mother's Anguish (A Mother's Tale) *Observer Magazine* 4.12.83; Octopus Books Ltd for extracts from *The World's Greatest Mistakes* ed Nigel Blundell; author's agents on behalf of the estate of the late Sonia Brownell Orwell, Martin Secker & Warbug Ltd and Harcourt Brace Jovanovich Inc for an extract from 'The Road to Wigan Pier Diary' by George Orwell in *The Collected Essays, Journalism and Letters of George Orwell* Vol 1 pg 218 copyright © 1968 by Sonia Brownell Orwell; Pan Books Ltd and Holt, Rinehart & Winston, Publishers for extracts from (World Atlas of Mysteries 1979) *The Mysterious World: An Atlas of the Unexplained* by Francis Hitching Copyright © 1978; Punch Publications Ltd for an extract from the review 'Solid Gold' by Dilys Powell *Punch* magazine March 1982; Syndication International Ltd for adapted extracts from the article 'Can You Think Yourself Well?' by Helen Speed *Woman* magazine 11.1.75; Syndication Sales for an adapted extract from the article 'Pioneer 10 pushes Beyond Goals, Into The Unknown' *International Herald Tribune* 5/5/83; the author's agents for an extract from *Picture Palaces* by Paul Theroux pp 268–269 (pub Hamish Hamilton); Times Newspapers Ltd for the adapted articles 'How divided twins grew up alike' by Alan Hamilton and Pearce Wright *The Times* 19.7.83, 'Enter G Man . . .' by Nicholas Wapshott *The Times* 17.3.83, 'The Times' Special Report on Information Technology' by Marcel Berlins *The Times* 14.1.82, 'The One-Man Factory of The Future' by Richard Brooks *The Sunday Times* 12.12.82, 'The Wealth in Health' by Malcolm Brown *The Sunday Times* 11.9.83, an extract from the article 'Smart 16 and worth £35,000 a year' by Alan Hamilton *The Times* 29.3.83, the abridged articles 'Walking laboratories in the nature-v-nature debate' by Alan Hamilton and Pearce Wright *The Times* 19.7.83, 'Arthur C. Clarke: fiction spilling over into fact' by Geoffrey Wansell *The Times* 4.11.82; the authors and author's agents for extracts from *Only One Earth* by Barbara Ward and Rene Dubos; author's agents on behalf of the Executors of the estate of H.G. Wells for an extract from the short story 'The Man Who Could Work Miracles' by H.G. Wells in *Selected Short Stories of H.G. Wells* (1962 Penguin Books).

Acknowledgements

We are grateful to the following for permission to reproduce copyright material:

Barnaby's Picture Library for pages 64 (bottom left) and 64 (bottom right); BBC Copyright for page 35; Camera Press Ltd for pages 48, 64 (top left) and 74; The J. Allan Cash Photolibrary for page 44 (top); Consumers' Association for page 52; The John Hillelson Agency Ltd, Stuart Franklin/Sygma for page 112; Michael Holford for page 34 (middle); photo by William Oliver/Jersey Wildlife Preservation Trust for page 92; adapted by permission of Justice of The Peace Ltd for page 29 (bottom); Keystone Press Agency for page 64 (middle); L.A.T. Photographic Ltd for page 132; Longman Photographic Unit for pages 16, 61, 62, 64 (top middle), 64 (middle left) and 64 (bottom middle); Mary Evans Picture Library for pages 34 (left) and 34 (right); from 'But It's My Turn To Leave You' by Mel Calman, Methuen London for page 27; from 'The Effluent Society' by Norman Thelwell, Methuen London for pages 32 and 50; Stills Department, National Film Archive for page 78; Northpix, Kevin Reid Ltd for page 8; Novosti Press Agency (APN) for page 18; adapted from 'Facts In Focus' compiled by the Central Statistics Office (Penguin Books, fifth edition 1980) page 136, Crown copyright 1972, 1974, 1975, 1978, 1980, Reprinted by permission of Penguin Books Ltd for page 105; Picturepoint-London for page 64 (top right); Major P.T.A. Plunkett for page 69 (top); Psychic News for page 69 (bottom); Punch Publications Ltd for page 6; Social Work Today, photo by Raissa Page/ Format for page 12; Peter Till for page 56; Times Newspapers Ltd for pages 7, 31 and 103; Topham Picture Library for page 93 (top); USIS (Paris) for page 108; adapted by permission of J. Whitaker & Sons Ltd for page 26; Yorkshire Television for page 39 (top).

Our special thanks to Clement Jocelyne Ltd for their help during location photography.

Artists
Peter Elson, John Fraser, June Jackson, Jane Laycock, David Mostyn, and Oxford Illustrators Ltd.

My mother is 80 now.
She ① me the strange story
of when she ② a child & she
③ to stay with her Aunt for the first
time. On arriving at the house she ④
the feeling that she ⑤ there before
after she ⑥ she ⑦ the way
to her bedroom although it
was a big rambling house & she
⑧ it previously. Everything ⑨
familiar. When she ⑩ her Aunt in
the kitchen, she ⑪ where to find everything
Up to this day she ⑫ why she ⑬
⑭ so at home in a place she
in before